# The Edge of
# COMPLEXITY

## THE WORKSHOP MANUAL FOR LEADERS AND MANAGERS

**EUR, ING., DR LEE E J STYGER**
MSc, PhD, CEng, CSci, CEnv, FIED, FIMMM, FICME, FCILT, REngDes, MIEA, SMSME

MANAGING BUSINESSES ON THE EDGE

**WFO**

# The Edge of
# COMPLEXITY

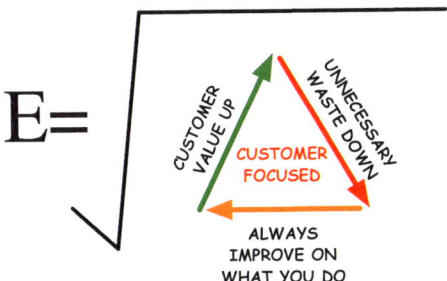

$$E = \sqrt{\phantom{xxxxx}}$$

CUSTOMER VALUE UP

UNNECESSARY WASTE DOWN

**CUSTOMER FOCUSED**

ALWAYS
IMPROVE ON
WHAT YOU DO

## MANAGING BUSINESS ON THE EDGE

### The Workshop Manual For Leaders and Managers

### The first in a three part series

**Eur, Ing., Dr Lee E J Styger**
MSc, PhD, CEng, CSci, CEnv, FIED, FIMMM, FICME, FCILT, REngDes, MIEA, SMSME

WFO

**World Foundry Organization Ltd**

**World Foundry Organization Ltd**
**London**

**WFO Publications**
The World Foundry Organization Ltd
Winton House
Lyonshall
Kington
Herefordshire
HR5 3JP
United Kingdom
Tel: +44 (0) 1544 3403326
Fax. 0044 1544 340332

First published 2014

**Disclaimer**
The material in this publication is in the nature of general comment only and does not represent professional advice. This material is not intended to provide specific guidance for specific organisations and should not be the basis for any decision on any matter. To the full extent permitted by law, the author and publisher disclaim any responsibility and liability to any person, arising directly or indirectly from any person acting or not acting based on information in this book.

Edited by Industrial Myth & Legend
ISBN9781503172005

FOR MY FAMILY

# CONTENTS

# ACKNOWLEDGEMENTS

I have been privileged and feel extremely fortunate to have been mentored by, worked with, consulted to and taught many inspiring, highly knowledgeable and wise people, all of whom have taught me much. Many people have contributed to this book over many decades of collaborative endeavour.

I would particularly like to thank the many cohorts of Executive Master of Business Administration students and Master of Business Administration students at the Sydney Business School, who have questioned and contributed, constructively commented and criticised, and provided valuable feedback on the philosophy, techniques and contents of this work over many lectures through many years.

I wish to thank all the people who have participated in the diagnostic process over the years who have brought their talent, ambition and skills to the task and courageously shown what can be done with the intention to create change. I would like to thank my colleagues at the University of Wollongong and in many other universities around the world, particularly the Hong Kong Polytechnic University, for their knowledge and learning that they so readily share.

To the many people in the World Foundry Organization who have participated in the creation of this book I would like to extend my sincerest gratitude and deepest respect for the expertise and professionalism you contribute both to your industry and management generally and for your the continuous efforts to improve business practices that have contributed to the realisation of this work.

Most of all I thank my family. Their support makes it all possible and they make it all worth doing. I am indebted to my research group members for their support and contributions both directly and indirectly to this work: Peter Critchley, Mark Edwards, Pradeepa Jayaratne, Fadi Kotob, Carol McGowan and Pauline Ross and also to my "associate research group", of all the Executive MBA students over the past five years who have contributed to this work in so many creative ways. Any errors or omissions in this work are mine alone. I have endeavoured to reference all work but if there are any oversights please let me know so that I can make amends.

# WORLD FOUNDRY ORGANIZATION

The World Foundry Organization (WFO) is the recognised centre of strategic foundry knowledge, designed to develop, enhance and improve the production of metal castings; through the latest technical and sustainable industry practices.

Through the involvement of the member associations in 30 countries, the WFO creates a network of technical knowledge and resource that is a vital tool to every foundry association, foundry and foundry worker throughout the world.

The WFO is a neutral body that represents the collective needs of the members on a global stage. The principal and important elements of the WFO are:

Executive Board Members

Member Organisations

Commissions

World Foundry Congresses and Technical Forums

This book is the work of the Sustainable Management Commission.

# FOREWORD

The Sustainable Management Commission is one of the professional commissions under the WFO to support the future of members around the world through the provision of best practices and best knowledge directed towards the ongoing development of the foundry industry.

For more than 25 years, I have seen Dr Lee Styger's transformative work in business reconfiguration and sustainable management. Lee combines industry experience with a professional and academic career to apply business optimising processes and outcomes in global industry leading organisations as well as in small businesses. There have been many requests by Members of the WFO, for the diagnostics presented by Lee at the WFO Technical Forum 2013 and we are pleased to present the diagnostics here in the first of a series of books on sustainable management.

Sustainability is about ensuring the long term continuity of organisations. While most commonly associated with social, environmental and economic issues, sustainability is also about improving competitive advantage in a new world business environment where a customer focus and collaborative approach enable opportunities for differentiation and the development of capabilities to change rapidly to meet changing market requirements. This book has been written as a workshop manual with practical tools and exercises to enable you to create a differentiated, customer focused, competitive and sustainable business.

Eur, Ing., Andrew Turner

# COMPLEXITY

## ABOUT THIS WORKSHOP MANUAL FOR LEADERS AND MANAGERS

A workshop manual for leaders and managers, this is a step-by-step guide to examining the strategic components of your organisation, how they work together and how they can be adjusted in order to maximise performance, get the results you want and take the organisation where you want it to go.

A short manual, it provides diagnostic tools for managers to develop a set of key data about their organisation and apply it to their strategic management responsibilities. The diagnostics are much needed in a rapidly changing business environment for generating up-to-date knowledge needed to manage the organisation at its best to achieve the organisational purpose.

The first in a trilogy provoking the development of alternative interpretations and perspectives of management practice and theory, this manual puts "best practice" in the context of your organisation so the most appropriate tools and techniques can be applied in the most successful way in your business. The first in a trilogy of work, COMPLEXITY is a guide for you to generate a strategy for attaining a successful sustainable organisation. A strategy that is specific to your organisation, based on understanding your business, your customers, your suppliers and whether your strategies are aligned. This manual is the accumulation of work that has been applied for over three decades in businesses, throughout the world, with transformative results.

# HOW TO USE THIS MANUAL

Designed to cut through the information overload of managers juggling the day-to-day tasks, this manual consists of six autonomous sections. Central to the manual are the diagnostics and these are supported by a narrative for understanding of the process. The sections of the manual can be approached in any order. To start on the diagnostics, it is possible to start directly at Act 1, Scene 2.

The manual uses the structure of a play. A prelude provides background. An overture provides an overview of the manual. Act 1 contains the three scenes of the diagnostics. A final prequel describes how we got to where we are today (i.e. "A long time ago in a galaxy far far away...").

A strength of completing the diagnostic process with colleagues is that resistance to change is often overcome as "the team" views "the problem", rather than each other "as the problem". A play reinforces the idea that this is a stage to challenge assumptions while working cooperatively, rather than a book to read. This is a manual that you "do"; that you play with. This manual requires you to be an actor, to participate by doing the diagnostics and to look at the "whole scene" in which your business activities operates. Most importantly, the process is dynamic - this manual doesn't deliver a one-size-fits-all, "you should do this" management fad but rather guides managers in developing alternative perspectives on the management trends and tools available, a method to use the knowledge derived from the best use of the best of these tools, an understanding of the business scene you are in now and, based on this, it is about enabling you to write the script going forward.

# ABOUT THE AUTHOR

## Eur, Ing., Dr Lee E J Styger

**MSc, PhD, CEng, CSci, CEnv, FIED, FIMMM, FICME, FCILT, REngDes, MIEA, SMSME**

Lee Styger (PhD) is Executive MBA Director at the Sydney Business School.

Lee has over three decades of international experience as a business leader, both in professional and private practice working for very large global industry leading organisations as well as very small start ups, and also as an educator, academic, engineer and author.

Best known as a creative thinker by many in professional practice, while perhaps regarded as a subversive thinker by many in academia, Lee's work revolves around developing others to challenge conventional wisdom by applying methods of examination and understanding, along with theory, to improve their own practices.

In addition to his work in business management and innovation, Lee is a named inventor on a number of patents in advanced technology areas diversifying from 3D printing to knowledge transfer and creative problem solving systems.

The Edge of COMPLEXITY


**THE WORKSHOP MANUAL FOR LEADERS AND MANAGERS**

# PRELUDE

## An Introduction to Complexity

The aim of this manual is to help leaders get the best from their organisations through determining a differentiated, sustainable and successful strategy specific to their organisation.

*In a free market only one business can be the cheapest,*
*the rest have to differentiate.*

The manual addresses this aim in several ways. Foremost are the diagnostics that help you decide where problems are and what work must be done to address these, as well as identify competitive opportunities. Around the diagnostics, detailed narrative provides information for improvement and, together with the forthcoming sequels, guidance for a complete overhaul of your organisation's competitive strategy.

It is hoped that this manual will enable leaders to see their business as a consultant would, develop alternative perspectives on how their business can compete in a complex business environment and use their specific knowledge of their business to set their own strategy for a successful sustainable business.

There are two reasons to be in business:
1. make money
2. make more money

There are two ways to make money:
1. process efficiency
2. product design

Process efficiency and product design are often considered to be addressed by innovation. Innovation, however, is not a bandaid. Successful innovation requires an understanding of what your business is because any innovation, theory or practice must be considered in the context of your organisation. The context of your organisation is the internal and external complex systems within which you operate and your organisation is a part of; including the suppliers and customers throughout your network. This will determine your process efficiency. This will determine your product design. This will determine your strategy. This will determine your innovation. This will determine your sustainable success. This context is what the diagnostics define.

The management of complexity is the new way that markets will be contested. To manage complexity requires understanding of the systems of our business. The legacies of the great thinkers of our industrial heritage, Ford, Deming, Ohno and Goldratt, to name a few, teach us that management of systems is key to success.

Conventional wisdom says that to stay in business requires cutting costs while providing customers with better quality and service. "Why isn't that enough?"

It is a lot more complex than that.

> *"When you make the complicated simple, you make it better,*
> *When you make the complex simple, you make it wrong.[1]"*

[1] Gray, D. (2009) ' quoted in Helen Hasan & Alanah Kazlauskas ed. Helen Hasan, *Being Practical with Theory: A Window into Business Research* (Theori, Faculty of Business, University of Wollongong, 2014), 79.

Complexity describes a system where there are lots of parts that are interconnected, interrelated, interdependent, interactive and influence each other and the whole system through their relationships. The whole is greater than the sum of its parts. The whole system cannot be understood by understanding each part. The relationships between the parts are as important as the parts themselves.

Business is complex. There is complexity both internally within our business and externally, beyond our businesses, with relationships between suppliers, customers and other forces that we can't necessarily even see, let alone control. The impact of the Global Financial Crisis of 2008 (GFC), is a compelling reminder of how interconnected to a wider environment organisations now are. There is a "wolf at your door".

This is not to say cutting costs and improving quality and service is wrong, however, without deeper knowledge of your organisational system, your suppliers, your customers, other external forces and how these all interact, the potential that can be realised by properly applying the "cutting costs while providing better quality and service to customers" concept will not be achieved. Instead, damage is done. Wrong assumptions lead to wrong decisions and a business, to its detriment, can become caught competing with a cost based strategy rather than a differentiated strategy.

Too often in businesses today, in the interests of administrative simplicity, the idea of a system, that is interdependence and cooperation for the achievement of a common result or goal, has been replaced with siloed and separated functions with independent targets. The wisdom of the giants of industry, which was based on the management of systems, has been corrupted to management by processes and specifications. Morphed mantras remain from their work, such as cutting costs and improving quality and service, but the systems view on which the mantra was based has been over-simplified or forgotten and with it the wisdom to ask which costs to be cut and which qualities and services to be improved.

*Sometimes you have to look back before you can look forward.*

It is time to again learn from the legacy of our industrial giants while understanding the complex systems of organisations today. This is not to say that administrative simplicity, processes and specifications that make the complicated simple, don't have their place. Too often, however, these "simplifications" have come to obscure and distort the understanding of the way the entire complex system functions, hide unchallenged assumptions and foster bureaucratic cultures that resist change. These factors, along with the exacerbation of the loss of the systems understanding that they cause, lead to making the wrong decisions from the wrong assumptions. When the assumptions are wrong and the entire system including the interrelationships with suppliers to customers isn't understood, opportunities for competitive advantage are lost and the inexorable slide starts to a cost-cutting strategy and a mediocre position in the market, if a position can be kept at all.

COMPLEXITY is about establishing the context of your organisation within this complex world. It is about developing the new perspective and skills needed to compete going forward. In the future, collaborative forces will be as important as competitive forces in creating a successful sustainable organisation.

A thorough awareness of the complexity of business today is essential to manage a change process to find opportunities, minimise vulnerability and move your organisation forward in a rapidly changing business environment.

## A Changed Business Environment and a Changed Business

The disruption of the GFC to the operating environment has made organisations more vulnerable, both through external factors such as less robust supply and availability of credit and, through internal factors such as loss of skills and knowledge through internal downsizing. Adding to the difficulties of increased vulnerability, businesses are also competing in an environment of higher uncertainty. The classic strategic analysis tools of business management, most accurate when the future is expected to be like the past and least accurate, yet most needed, when the future is not expected to be like the past, are unreliable in the uncertain environment in which businesses now operate. Many businesses are lost and in need of a compass and a map to determine where they are, as much as how to move forward and, yet, are trying to get on with "business as usual".

To remain competitive, the challenge now is to understand fully the "new world order", the degree of interconnectedness, or complexity, that exists in the business environment today and the vulnerability and unpredictability that results from this complexity. To move forward in the most competitive way we need to know where we are; audit what we have, understand the complexity and design our business to move forward using the best tools available for the uncertainties of the environment.

Our businesses, too, are simply not the same as the businesses we had before the crisis and there is a need to understand how they work today. It is vital to accept that the business we have now is systematically different to the way it was before the crisis and it will need nurturing in a fundamentally different way, if we are to sustain, nurture and grow our businesses and remain competitive into the future. In many cases, however, we are basing the decisions of today on the rules and tools of yesterday. Even if our current organisation carries the same brand as before, its structure and the system in which it operates, has transformed from what we knew and managed well, into something new and operationally different. The parameters of business have effectively changed, "square has become triangle" but we are still trying to manage our new "triangle" organisation by the the rules of the old square organisation (see Figure P.1).

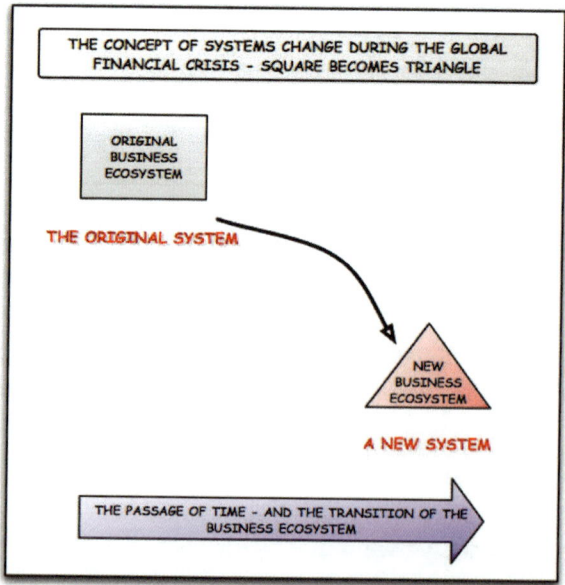

*Figure P.1 - A Schematic of the Changing Parameters of Business as a Result of the Global Financial Crisis - "Square Becomes Triangle"*

Managing in complexity requires a systems focus than encompasses a customer focus. This "customer focus" extends to having better knowledge of end customers and their needs and preferences, even if your business is not with the end customer. Customer focus is now about all of the network of supply working together on adding value to end customers and reducing non-value adding waste and costs in the whole system.

Managing in complexity requires a focus on your customer responsiveness. Customer responsiveness is the capability of your organisation and its network to change quickly to meet new market demands.

Managing in complexity requires new levels of communication throughout your organisation's complex system so all the system is engaged in the customer focused and customer responsive approach to business.

Complexity decreases the amount of control a manager has over their organisation while increasing uncertainty and vulnerability. Control is decreased because, with a high degree of interconnectedness, change in the wider system, even a distant part of the system, can have an unpredictable influence. Uncertainty is increased because change is rapid and this makes forecasts unreliable. Vulnerability is increased because many organisations are still recovering from the last crisis and less able to cope with uncertainty and this is exacerbated by less control. Complexity, however, can also increase opportunities for diversity and resilience if it is understood and there is a strategic design to best use the complexity to achieve the organisation's purpose.

Managing complexity is the contemporary leader's challenge and responsibility. Efforts at reducing or simplifying the complexity will only move or change the complexity rather than resolve it. Rather, managing complexity through knowing your system, increasing communication, using interconnections with suppliers and customers for competitive advantage through collaboration, communication, adding value through knowledge and increased customer focus can turn complexity into your greatest opportunity (see Figure P.2).

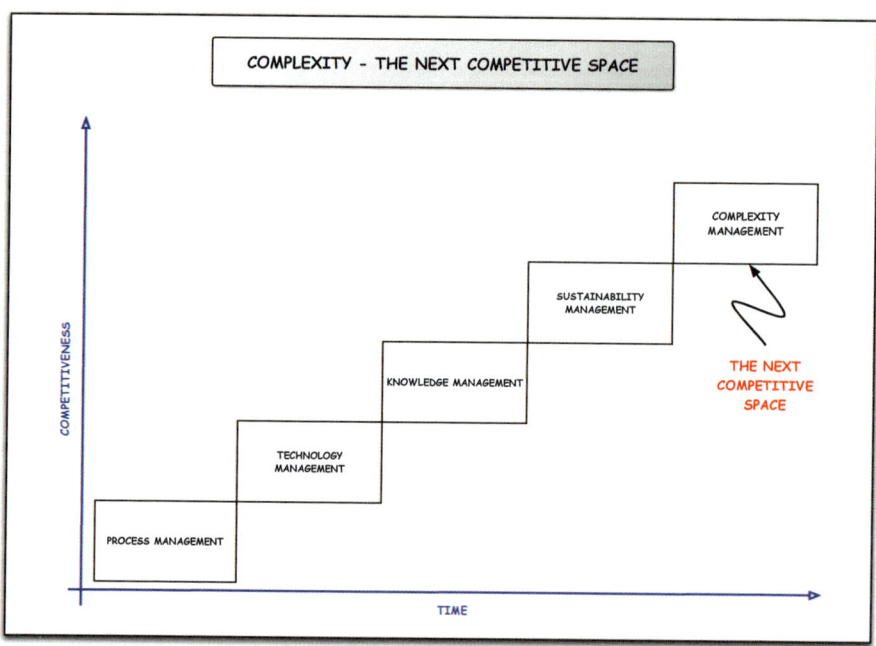

*Figure P.2 The Leadership Challenge of Managing a Changing Competitive Space*

COMPLEXITY is about challenging assumptions, regaining the understanding of your business's whole system and understanding the application of the wisdom of the great thinkers of business, not the morphed assumptions and management fads from over-simplification of this wisdom, to remain competitive and profitable in today's business environment. Cost cutting doesn't build business. To build business requires investment and innovation based on the five coordinates for navigating and managing a business edge in uncertain space: who is your customer, why do they buy from you, where is your organisation now, where can your organisation go and how is your organisation going to get there. COMPLEXITY is a manual for establishing these coordinates for your organisation.

# OVERTURE

## Complexity and the Context of Your Business

How many of us have read and re-read the great management books of our time but we are still not wearing different hats when we think, are still working closer to an 80 hour week than a four hour week, are still taking more than one minute to manage and, are working both smarter and harder than ever?

These great management books are indeed great and inspirational in their content. Many have come from rigorous research and/or triggered the same but, often, the concepts or messages of these works aren't applied or fast forgotten in our businesses because, to successfully apply best practice, we are required to put these transformational practices into the context of our organisation and what we do professionally on a day-to-day basis. An axiom of one size or solution fits and cures all of the problems we face, is flawed. Any change must be made with consideration of the reality of the business you have already got and where it already is (i.e. applied to the context of your business). Understanding your business and how your business is interrelated with the other businesses that are your suppliers and customers, is the essential first step in mapping where your business can go and applying the powerful management tools available to get there.

COMPLEXITY is the first of a series of manuals designed to take business leaders and managers through a process of focusing on their business, mapping where it is at present, where it can successfully move forward to and how it can get there. Figure O.1 illustrates that COMPLEXITY is about including the context of your actual business both with the theories we have inherited from industrial giants such as W. Edwards Deming, Taiichi Ohno, Eliyahu M. Goldratt and Henry Ford; that are based on understanding business systems and continuous improvement, and with the inspirations of the modern "best practice" management tools and techniques.

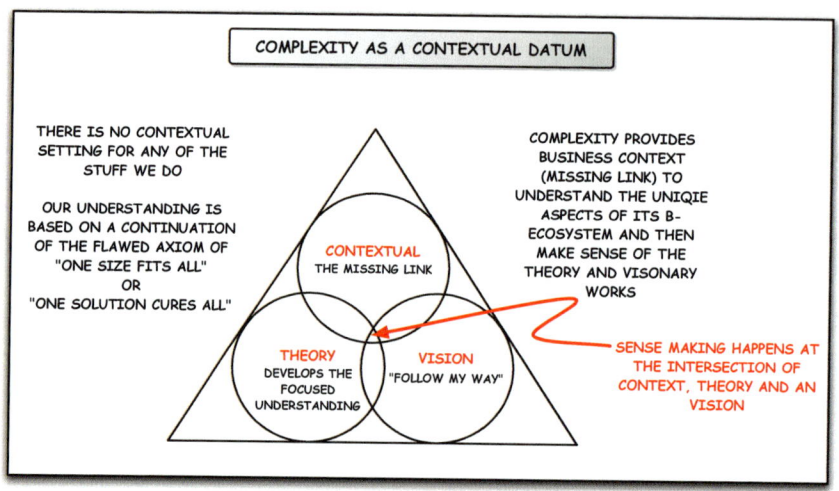

*Figure O.1 - COMPLEXITY as a Contextual Datum*

COMPLEXITY provides a set of diagnostics, using the Systems Audit Approach (Figure O.2), to provide the specific knowledge of your own business that is needed to make sense of many of the theories, practices and "inspirations" (i.e. ideas, opportunities and management tools) presented to us. COMPLEXITY offers a dynamic datum, but requires work from you, the reader, because to make sense of risk or opportunity within the context of your business, you have to define and understand your business dynamics now and, with the passage of time, continually change, redefine and re-understand your business dynamics.

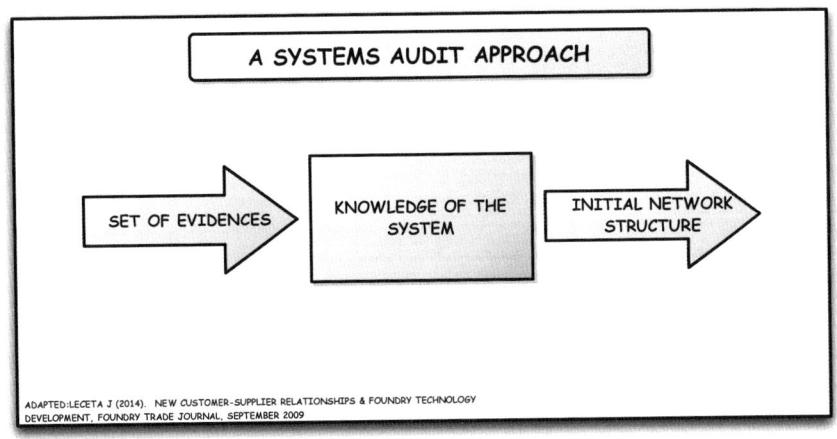

*Figure O.2 COMPLEXITY as a Systems Audit Approach*

There is no dispute that the business environment of today is characterised by rapid change and uncertainty. To lead and manage in a rapidly changing environment requires a clear picture of what is happening, how it happens, where it happens, who does it, the connections, the weaknesses and the potential opportunities, not just within your organisation but also beyond its walls. This understanding needs to extend to the suppliers, customers and markets of your business.

Contemporary businesses are often being managed with an almost opposite approach. Bureaucratised divisions of labour and budgets have instilled an inward looking, cost-down focus, rather than an outward looking focus on effectively achieving the purpose of the business, increasing profits and retaining and winning customers who pay for what you do. Increased specialisation and separation of departments, with a management focus on short-term targets, has resulted in little consideration being given to the business as part of a much larger system of interrelated businesses and, for many leaders, the concept of understanding and managing the business in relation to the external forces is no longer clearly defined or understood. This increases the vulnerability of a business in a rapidly changing environment.

Businesses today operate in a complex adaptive system. Put simply, a complex adaptive system describes a system of many integrated and interdependent relationships in which the whole is bigger than the sum of its parts and a change in one, even seemingly unrelated, distant and even unseen part, can have unexpected and unpredictable consequences for other parts.

Complex is not about how complicated or difficult something is but describes the involvement of a lot of parts interconnected in many ways that make up a whole. Something can be complex without being complicated but many things that are complicated are also often complex. When something is complex to take out parts without understanding all the interrelationships might stop the whole from working properly. Complexity theories are still evolving and recently, a social-ecological systems theory has been proposed to extend the systems ecology and complexity theories to directly include social concerns such as wellbeing considerations (see Figure O.3). These wellbeing concerns are also an important part of business and part of the considerations raised in the sequels to this manual.

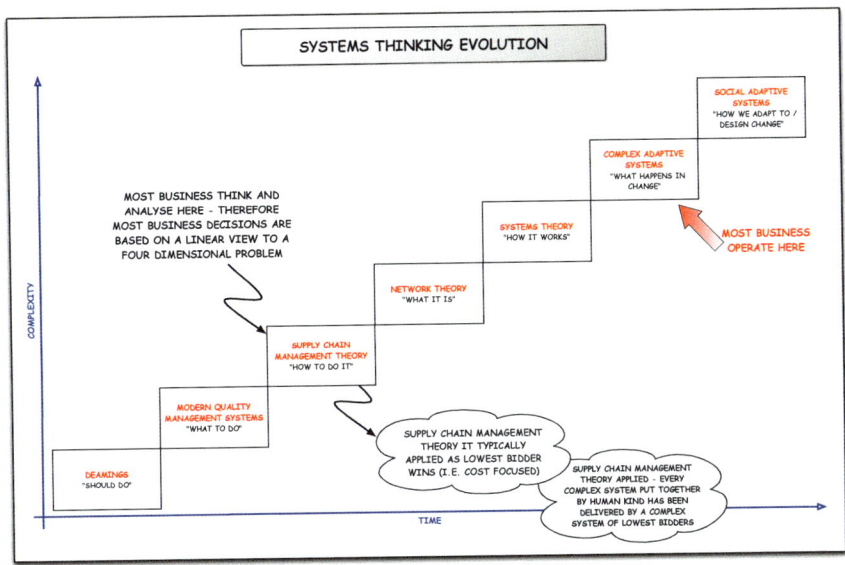

*Figure O.3 - Systems Thinking Evolution*

This work, however, is not intended as an academic argument about the definition of complexity but, rather, about the need for management processes in a complex adaptive system that are flexible, innovative and adaptive, that can respond effectively to the unexpected and that allow leaders to create change, rather than only react to change. In ecology, the term ecosystem is used to describe the important interrelationships in nature and, as this is a familiar concept that readily reminds us that even a small change in any one aspect of an ecosystem can change the entire ecosystem, the term b-ecosystem has been adopted here to describe the highly interdependent and interrelated business environment that exists today.

If business leaders regard their businesses as a b-ecosystem (i.e. holistically) and manage with this concept guiding the way they treat their b-ecosystem, as they have been taught to do by Deming and many other industry giants, they can achieve significant cost savings and quality improvements. For many, however, the concept of viewing the business as a b-ecosystem takes them well outside of their comfort zone and personal short term agendas. The problem is that traditional business teaching and thinking forces a one dimensional or myopic approach to decision making within a "b-ecosystem", that is continually and rapidly changing.

Ignorance or denial of the b-ecosystem keeps businesses well below the intellectual level of their competitors and ultimately drives them into oblivion. Business must operate within the conceptual construct of a b-ecosystem if they are to survive, prosper and leave a positive legacy into the future. This conceptual evolution of management thought towards a holistic "ecosystem" approach is illustrated above in Figure O.4, reproduced from Figure P.2 in the Prelude.

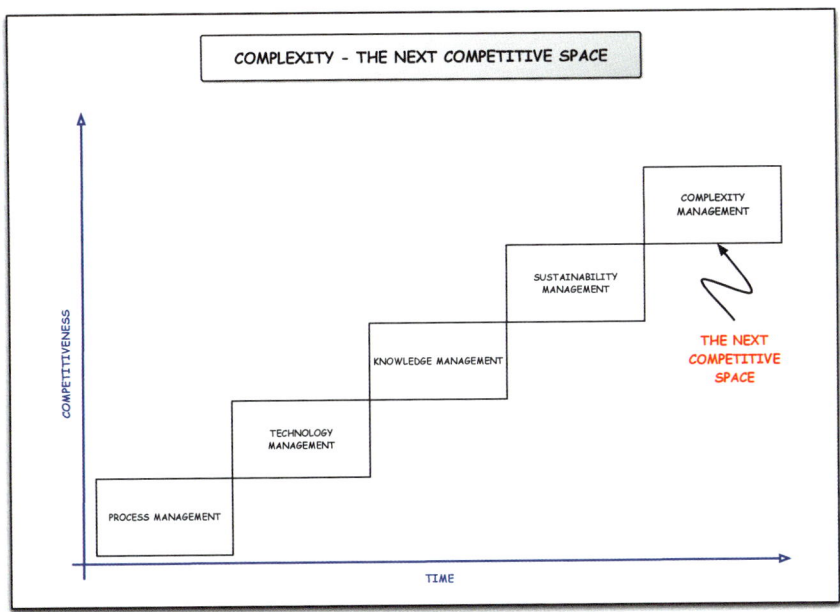

*Figure O.4 The Leadership Challenge of Managing a Changing Competitive Space*

An approach to business based on understanding systems is certainly not new. It cannot be stated often enough that this is the message of the great industrial giants who bequeathed contemporary business to us. One of the greatest failings has been to ignore or marginalise the works of former industrial giants and segment businesses to the point of over bureaucratised stagnation. Deming's philosophy was based around competitive advantage and improving the strategic position of companies through the business ecosystem. Over time, and in common with much of the great wisdom of the age, his work has become marginalised to monitoring the flow of worth through the system and not managing the system itself. An "A" versus "B" comparison was offered by some of his Japanese contemporaries in the 1970's and it is as applicable today as it was then. This Deming's focus on quality as opposed to cost comparison is illustrated in Figure O.4.[2]

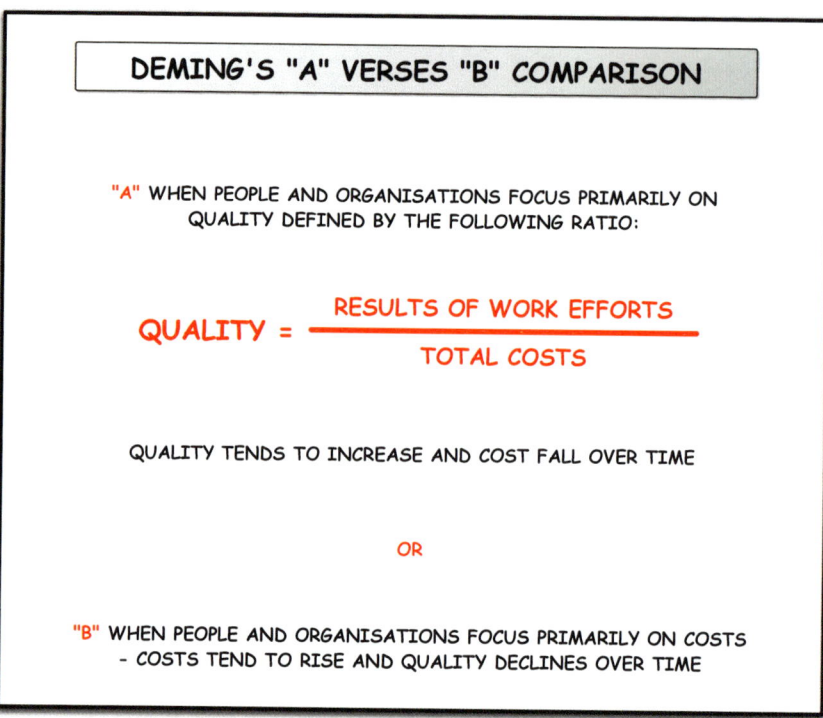

*Figure O.5 - Deming's "A" verses "B" Comparison*

The language of business and of these past industrial giants has been corrupted and morphed into a nonsensical mantra (see Figure O.5). We have been taught by modern management practices to segment and silo what we do. The concept of the business being a b-ecosystem of itself and interacting with larger b-ecosystems around it, has been lost and with it the understanding of where the contribution (aka real value) is.

[2] Wikipedia, *W. Edwards Deming*, <http://en.wikipedia.org/wiki/W._Edwards_Deming> accessed 5 November 2014

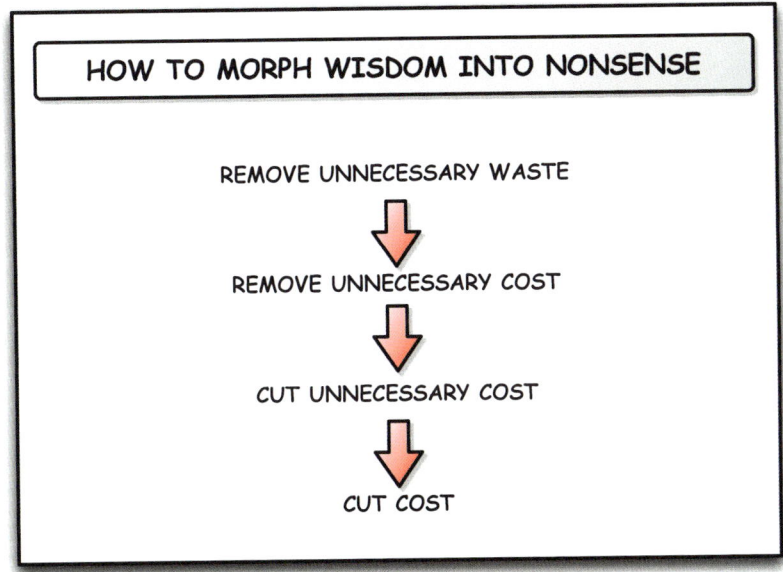

*Figure O.6 - The Morphing of the Wisdom of Industry Giants into Nonsensical Mantra*

It is worth repeating that cutting costs does not build business. You cannot save your way to success. To challenge the assumptions and misunderstandings that often underlie common practice, due to the morphing of wisdom into mistaken mantras, and to return to the underlying tradition of achieving business growth and viability based on understanding systems and continuous improvement, leaders require thinking processes that take them outside the silo's of specialisation and separation, outside the box of management fads, trends and short-term targets and also outside the organisation's walls to do an up-to-date check of the exact state of their business. Leaders require a process that can capture the dynamics of business. This process, itself, must be continuous without being overly time consuming.

COMPLEXITY provides such a process for business leaders who are now willing, waiting and wanting to differentiate and remove their organisation from the grey commoditised mediocrity resulting from a cheap cost-centred strategy. It offers a provocative, alternative view of what happens when there is insatiable copying of management trends and fads of business, by myopic leadership, who do not even slow down for a nano-second to ponder what happens when they destroy knowledge capital within their organisations when they cut costs and reduce staff or, indeed, come the good times if they will ever be able to recover.

We are told that the greatest sign of madness is doing the same thing over and over again and expecting a different outcome. This, however, is what appears to be happening within the business environment. Many of our leaders typically do not lead anymore but follow dangerous fashions and trends intended to deliver greater returns and security but that all too often fail because they are not applied with consideration of the context of the business and instead uncontrollably drive businesses to a commoditised position.

While complexity increases uncertainty and vulnerability, paradoxically, it also provides opportunities for diversity and resilience if it is understood and leadership is flexible in its approach to find innovative ways to use the complexity to further the business's purpose. This requires an understanding of the b-ecosystem, however, in many businesses the picture of what, how and who is interrelated is sketchy at best. Very few see the "big picture" of their business, their customers, their suppliers, their competitors and how they are interrelated and the space they operate in. As such, very few businesses are using the opportunities of complexity in the b-ecosystem to mitigate risk and expand competitive advantage.

*Knowing your business, how it fits into a b-ecosystem and how to differentiate to delight your customer is imperative to remain competitive and operational.*

## The Relationship Between Risk and Growth

There is a tendency to see the size of a business as an important consideration in the reduction of risk. Certainly, the risk appetite of a business reduces significantly as it grows (see Figure O.6). Aversion to risk, however, creates a conservative decision culture that becomes supported and normalised by policy and procedure. This in turn drives a business to the safe middle ground market, typically characterised as commodity and cost/price centric where the majority of the players in the market group around similar product or service offerings. The result is usually the emergence of a hyper-competitive environment exemplified by low margins for larger effort. Figure O.7 illustrates how organisational growth is typically accompanied by a decreasing organisational risk acceptance profile.

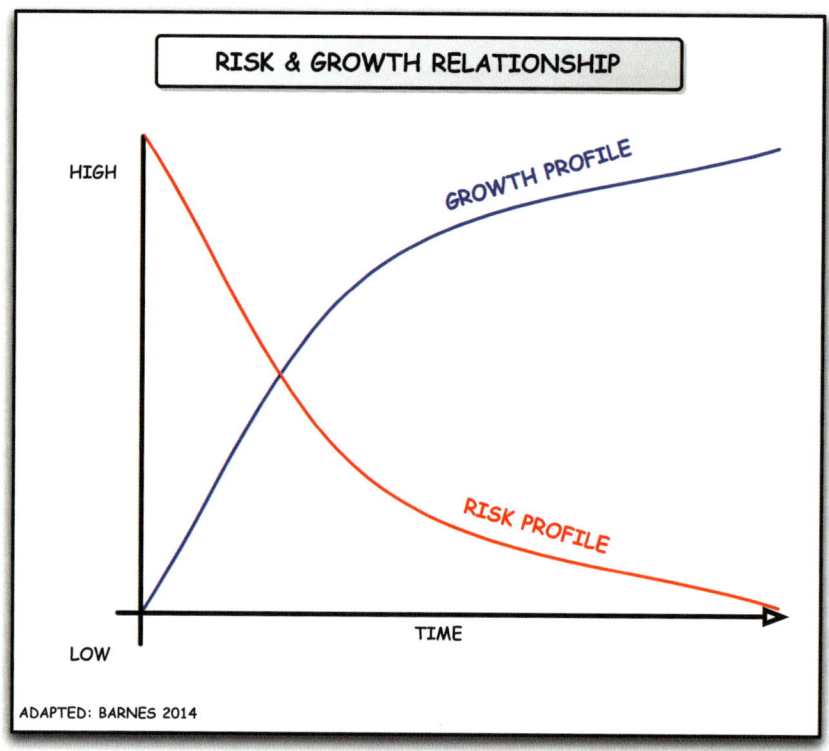

*Figure O.7 - Concept of Risk and Growth Relationships*

Commoditisation does not guarantee market dominance. In many cases, commoditisation opens up distinct and alternative lucrative markets (niches), where the volume player cannot go due to the forced mediocrity of a portfolio of products and services designed for the middle ground, as is demanded in commoditised markets.

Differentiation by the incumbent players is, therefore, perceived as difficult and considered high risk by mainstream management and, as such, precludes them from decisions that could generate alternative competitive strategies. This in turn opens up niches in the market for newcomers who are more agile and more risk accepting (see Figure O.8). Success of the newcomer creates a paradigm step change in market dynamics that can undermine the dominant players, and it often why paradigm change comes from outside of an industry or the recognised b-ecosystem.

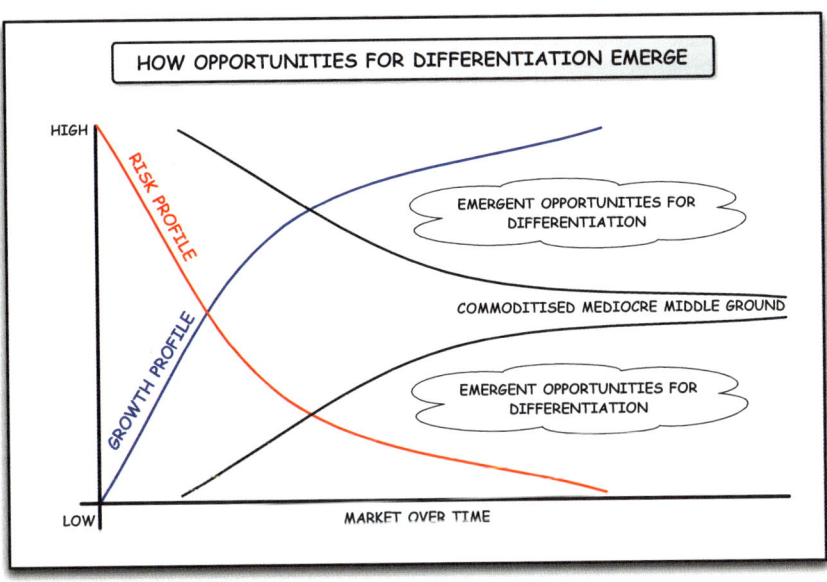

*Figure O.8 - Concept of How Opportunities for Differentiation Emerge*

*Put simply, because much classical management theory is based on a one size fits all principle, it excludes notions of differentiation as cost generating and strategically courageous. As such, businesses follow fashion and don't create or innovate their own future.*

To operate in a commoditised market, a business must follow the rules of that market and surrender many alternative opportunities. Typically, leadership is relegated and "management by policy" prevails. This generates institutional and cross-institutional consensus. Consensus leads to conformity and drags a business further away from the hope of finding a new way via differentiation. Remarkably, the principle of "last mover advantage"[3] prevails, further demanding a cost centric commoditised business model. However, in a cost centric commoditised market, only one company can be the cheapest and the rest are forced to do something different - differentiate - and this is where the rich paradox of modern business converges and the new, complex, competitive battle ground is drawn.

**Differentiation**

Many businesses typically approach differentiation from a perspective of trying to achieve market or world domination. This doesn't happen and is the wrong approach. A market doesn't need to be dominated to be successfully contested. Any system will grow to maximum capacity and then there is a natural cycle where internal or external forces will cause that market dominance to collapse, unless it is a differentiated market where first mover dynamics take precedence and this moves the business closer to the customer and 'customised' differentiation. It is then difficult for any would-be substitute player to break the bond between your business and your customer.

A differentiation strategy does require knowledge and leadership as opposed to management by process and specifications. The difficulty in

---

[3] In a cost sensitive market there is little opportunity for investment. All activities within an organisation are price driven and the organisation is forced to hold onto existing product and assets for as long as possible further driving the need for conformity - i.e. they cannot afford to be first to market with any product.

making this change is exacerbated by the certainty that the business environment is changing at a rate never before experienced and in the need to keep up, many businesses are having to make decisions fast and often without any reference point or market intelligence. As a result, safer strategies have been adopted. Technology, for example, that should be an enabler has often become the substitute for differentiation. Businesses have lost contact with themselves and their customers. Rampant desocialisation of the business process, through siloing, outsourcing and even by the reliance on e-communication, has led to near criminal devaluation of intellectual assets. Without knowledge and leadership, as opposed to information and management, solutions provision has, typically, become a quick fix and the business ecosystem has been systematically "bandaided" for far too long.

Alarmingly, businesses now react to their environment instead of pre-acting and creating their own future. Big picture strategic thinking has become small thinking tactical maneuvering. Markets are no longer designed, commanded and controlled but, rather, squabbled over in skirmishes, where the price paid by heavy casualties on both sides fails to deliver any measurable increase in territory. Categorization is good for exploitation but bad for complex systems and situations and periods of change. Markets are now recognised as rapidly changing and yet our decision capability is hamstrung by conflicting frameworks and principles typically focused at the departmental level and not the b-ecosystem in its entirety.

Where and how change happens in a business or ecosystem is not intuitive. For example, over many years of observation Kerzner (2006) is of the opinion that those persons in the organisation who should be the leaders of change are typically those who are most likely to oppose change the most venomously (see Figure O.9). This might be a function of the archaic and often myopic siloed management structures that force cost accounting and remedial performance management measures.

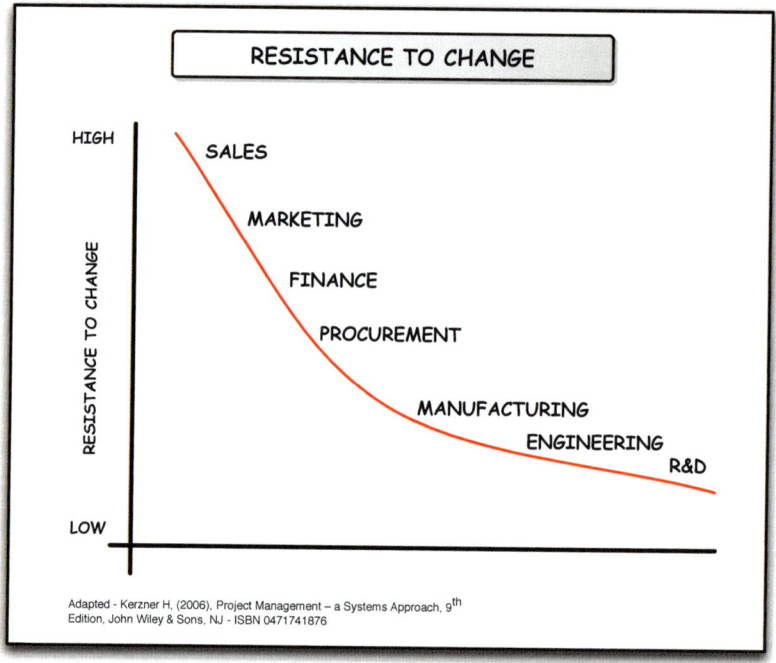

*Figure O.9 - Resistance to Change within Business Functions*

I've always said that I want to write a book and title it Zen and The Art of Car Parking, which is an unashamed homage to Robert Pirsig's critically acclaimed work Zen and the Art of Motorcycle Maintenance. The title was inspired by many a Saturday shopping spree hitting car parks where people are trying to find and fight for spaces as close to the doors to the mall as possible. My modus operandi has always been, albeit against ferocious objection from my family in most cases, to actually look for a space as far away from the doors as possible. Sometimes as close to the dumpster or service entrance as possible. Why do I do this? I argue that the place furthest from the doors, the place closest to the dumpster, especially in the Australian hot summer, is the least likely place that anyone would want to park and, therefore, the most likely place that I'm going to find a parking space rapidly and without the hassles or the fight close to the door. On a Christmas Eve a few years ago, the notion of Zen and the Art of Car Parking and the philosophy of:

*To find your space - you first have to look in unusual places.*

became enriched within the folklore of my own family and it's become almost a mantra for private practice and my educational work ever since.

Businesses can no longer follow the pack, no longer hide behind a one-size-fits-all management fad but, rather, have to step out and have to differentiate. To be successful, most businesses need to find a place that is unusual.

In many businesses this has already been recognised and there is a cry for innovation, however, while businesses actively suffocate creativity and disregard innovation as a tool within their own organisational structures, customer and supplier engagement practices, employee role descriptions and reimbursement arrangements, knowledge utilisation and retainment practices and so on, the full potential benefits of innovation will not be realised and many in the organisation will continue to regard innovation as an unnecessary provocateur of change and an evil cost generator.

To create a future we must understand the past. Before we change something we must understand the wider context within which that "something" exists. Using a systems audit approach, the diagnostic tools in Act 1, together with the strategic insights developed in the sequels, provide tools with which to navigate through the complexities of ever changing space and create a future for our organisations based on sustainable differentiation (see Figure O.10).

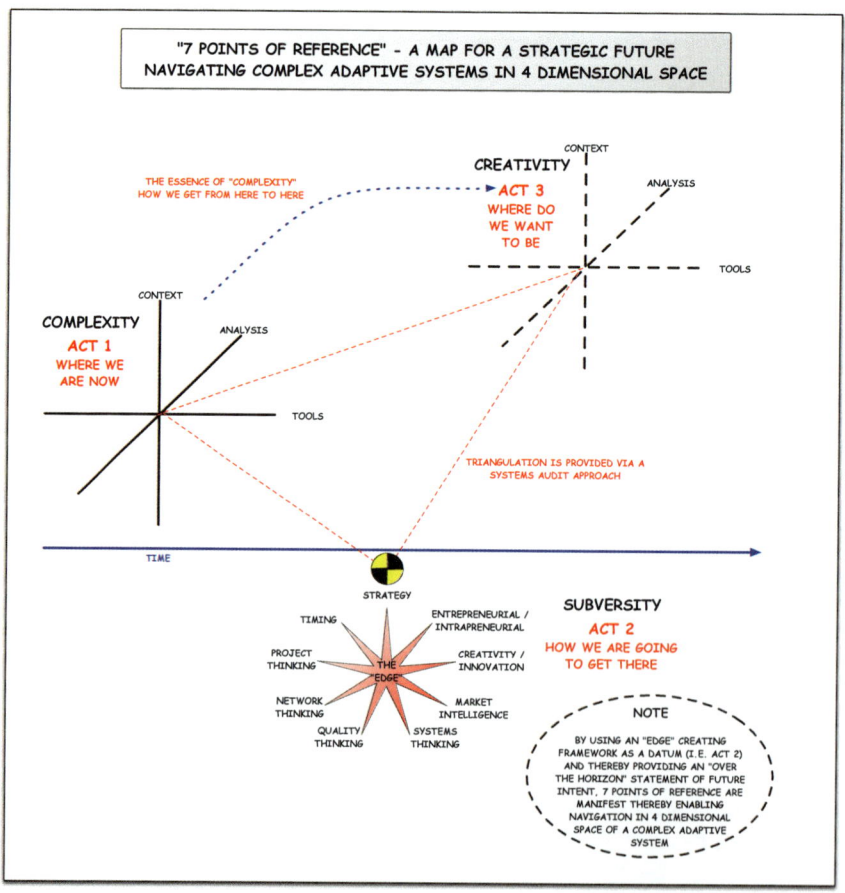

*Figure O.10 - Navigating Complex Adaptive Systems in Four Dimensional Space*

# ACT 1

## EVALUATING CURRENT BUSINESS DYNAMICS

**ACT 1 - SCENE 1**

**EVALUATING THE CURRENT BUSINESS DYNAMIC -**

**WHERE IS YOUR BUSINESS NOW?**

COMPLEXITY is specifically about your business. Most business books specialise on a topic then generalise to all businesses. This is the first of a series of manuals to guide managers through a process of generating relevant management data specifically from their actual business, understanding the data in the context of their actual business environment and using this understanding to design and manage the profitable, competitive and sustainable future they envision for their business. Figure 1.1.1 illustrates the three step process provided by this series.

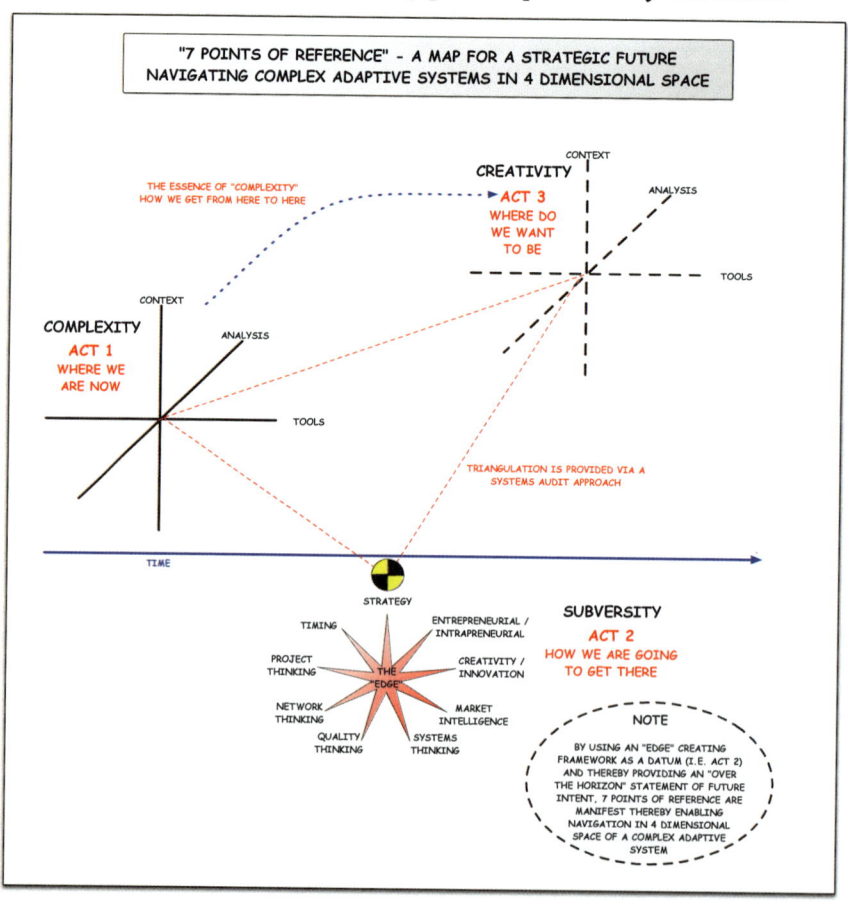

*Figure 1.1.1 - Navigating Complex Adaptive Systems in Four*
*Dimensional Space*

Act 1, the manual which you are reading now, generates the information about where your business is today. Act 2, the second manual in the series, is about developing a strategic framework to determine where the best place is for your business to go. Act 3, the third manual in the series, takes you through a process to map a way forward.

Because this is about your business a systems audit approach[4] is used to generate the information about your business that you need. This data forms the basis for triangulation of the reference points of "Where is your business now?", "Where is your business going?" and "How is your business going to get there?". It is important to note that the answers to these questions are found from the data generated about your business. This is a process of working with what your business is; not a general one-size-fits-all approach. Act 1 generates the data about where your business is now, through a set of 26 diagnostic tools that you are asked to complete. This is work, however, it also works. These diagnostics have been deployed over many years with transformative and positive results in a wide range of organisations.

The response from many of the people who have participated in the use of the diagnostics to date is that, although initially the theory or the ideas behind the diagnostics appears a little dry, after the implementation stage major gaps and/or areas of improvement are typically highlighted, that in turn create a catalyst for further investigation and improvement. The process becomes inspiring. Perhaps one of the strengths of these

[4]James R. Evans & William M. Lindsay, *An Introduction to Six Sigma & Process Improvement*, Cengage Learning, CT, 2005; Tillmann Bohme, Paul Childerhouse, Eric Deakins, Andrew Potter, Denis.R. Towill, Why diagnosis supply chain uncertainty?, *Operations Managment*, Vol.34 No. 3, 2008

diagnostics, in this chaotic world, is that they force the once common practice of considered and reflective focus on the issue at hand not a "shoot form the hip" reaction from the participant.

The diagnostics are the culmination of 30 years work experience and were developed as tools for both business and process improvement during my career in professional and private practice. Broadly speaking, my industry career has been in the areas of business reconfiguration, innovation and change; for businesses ranging from very large global industry leaders to very small start ups. In my academic career, I continue to work with executives, from a similarly broad range of organisations, in these and other areas.

To put it succinctly, my own career has been a transition from, initially, being occupied in designing the stuff companies sell to later designing the companies to sell the stuff (see Figure 1.1.2).

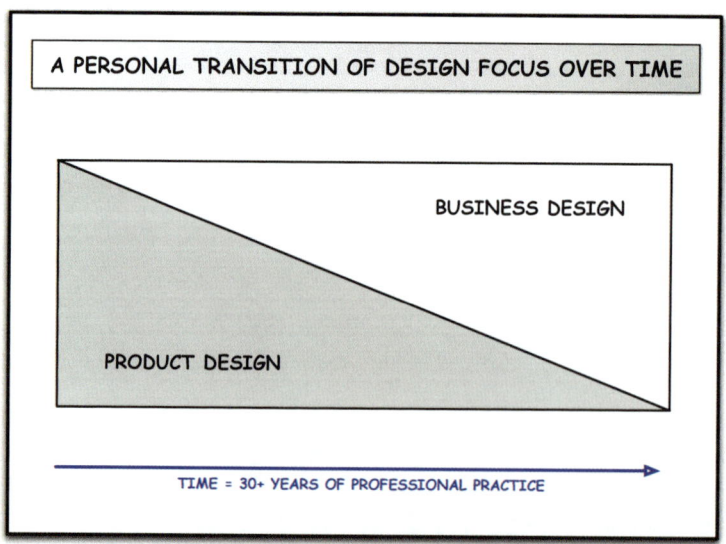

*Figure 1.1.2 - My Personal Transition of Design Focus Over Time*

Due to some unique roles at unique institutions around the world, I have been fortunate to be associated with many businesses and develop from a specialist in a single, traditional discipline, to a career with a longevity and breadth that provides unconventional insights that challenge many more commonly held views.[5]   I have been involved with businesses in growth, some that were in decline, many of which have the normal ups and downs of everyday life.  The motivation behind COMPLEXITY has been one of responding to business requests for guidance at a time when business seems to dealing with issues of survival in unprecedented change.

**Creating Change**

COMPLEXITY is a  manual to guide how we react to change or perhaps now, moving forward, how we preact to change, that is create change and take control our own futures in an uncertain environment.

A misattribution to Darwin states that:

*"It is not the strongest of the species that survive, nor the most intelligent, but the ones most responsive to change."*[6]

This insight is highly relevant to understanding business today in this rapidly changing and complex business environment.  While it challenges common business teaching and thinking, in that we typically assume that

---

[5] Hence the accolade by some that I am a subversive thinker!

[6] The Darwin Correspondence Project,<http://www.darwinproject.ac.uk/one-thing-darwin-didnt-say> University of Cambridge, 2014

size is proportional to stability and profitability (i.e. strength) and that the larger the organisation the more chance there is for survival, this is not necessarily the case because, in todays business environment, where it is possible to go "nowhere fast", it is the speed of response to a given situation that can often mean the difference between longevity or not.[7]

Business fashions dictate the trend for centralised or decentralised structures and this is cyclical over time and industry sector. The more a business is centralised the less agile it is. The larger the business the larger and more complex the business ecosystem becomes and the less potential there is for maneuvering. Risk adverse policies drive decision making and the resultant strategies drive many such businesses to the common middle ground ("safe mediocrity").[8]   The more markets converge (i.e. companies move to the middle ground and become a larger centralised cluster) the more opportunity opens up for agile companies to take differentiated spaces and fill niche markets left by the centralisers.

A more recent twist in this dynamic is that global communications and connections technology (the Internet) has allowed what were once small and somewhat uninviting niches to become themselves clustered around the technology enabler and now offer markets of extreme interest and opportunity.[9]

---

[7] This is why large organisations try to emulate the actions of small organisations

[8] Safe in this case denotes a stagnant situation where there is little hope of agile movement or repositioning in times of trauma

[9] S. Godin, *Purple Cow*, Penguin Books, London, 2005

## Building Competitive Advantage Through the Business Ecosystem

These niche areas are a reminder that businesses today operate in a complex adaptive system (CAS), that functions with characteristics such as niches, much like an ecosystem. As described in the Overture, a complex adaptive system is not about whether a system is complicated but, rather, describes a system with energy flows through many integrated, interrelated, interdependent parts that can have unexpected and unpredictable influences on each other. The term 'ecosystem' is an ecological term to describe complexity in natural systems. As the term "ecosystem" is more familiar than "complex adaptive system", for the purpose of describing the concept of complexity as it relates to business, the term b-ecosystem, for "business ecosystem", has been adopted in this work.

Complexity, if understood, can be a tool for competitive advantage; as niche market opportunities demonstrate. Complexity, if misunderstood, increases vulnerability and uncertainty. This will be further discussed, particularly in terms of supply networks, in Act 3 after the opportunities being identified in your business through the diagnostics in Act 2. The foundation for this is Act 1 which is about establishing the b-ecosystem of your business as the tool for building competitive advantage.

## Challenging the Old Approach

A gap has become apparent where the management mantras and practices of yesterday are not necessarily fitting the requirements of modern practice and importantly modern business dynamics. This might be due to a lag time for theoretical principles becoming mainstream in industry, but what I've noticed is that:

*We are managing the issues of today based on the practices and realities of yesterday at the same time that we have, at best, corrupted the wisdom of a systems practice of business, developed by the giants of our industrial heritage, into discrete processes for optimising isolated functions rather than the overall results of the business.*

This is troubling because, if allowed to continue, there is no sustainability and we will not leave a legacy for future generations and we might even see a decline in the common standards of humanity into the future.

Short term management mantra has left a long-term toxicity in organisations, where the people charged with maintaining the ecosystem now want to find better work, instead of making their work better. We can all build our "New Jerusalem" in our own dreams, perspectives and ambitions of success and power, yet few of us are prepared to improve the current "Jerusalem" from the inside out and, in doing so, improve the collective position of our entire b-ecosystem. Yet, it is this that we are charged to do as stewards and persons of responsibility within our organisations.

One of the inhibitors of change is that many organisations are living off a dangerous legacy of shadowed walled thoughts, assumptions and habitual actions. This internal cultural legacy is often based on incomplete market intelligence, old school learning and management neglect.

One of the key points of feedback, from previous participants of the initial set of diagnostics is this culture of shadow walling. Shadow walls, or the concepts of shadow walls, are those axioms of belief or cultural norms or limitations, that organisations place around themselves and others. Typically, shadow walls are as high as real walls but you can't see them. Even when you hit them straight on, they are invisible but stop efforts for change and progression in so many ways. Shadow walls hold us back, they kept us contained and they imprison us in today or, indeed, yesterday, instead of opening up the future. This concept is discussed again in Scene 3 where we talk about the idea of the limitations of cultural belief sets within the organisation and how these can be the real inhibitor of change for so many organisations.

Shadow wall thinking is particularly dangerous for our businesses because of the assumptions that it hides. Conclusions drawn in any situation will often depend on assumptions already made. When the assumptions are wrong, conclusions are often, at best, distorted or flawed. These assumptions are not usually articulated or even recognised, much less challenged.

The potential negative impact of this is likely to increase. This is because one of the greatest inhibitors of the 21st Century business environment is the contradiction between data driven decision making and an over abundance of low quality data. While the numbers generated from the data are generally correct, the assumptions behind the interpretation of the data are too often wrong and this is likely to get far worse with the uptake of big data mining and computational probability (i.e. the algorithms will drive everyone using them to the same point - middle ground). We exist in a world of information overload where there is little respect given for mastery and the optimal pinnacle of decision leverage - wisdom (derived through experience). This is illustrated in Figure 1.1.3, "The Hierarchy of Wisdom" model, which illustrates that while we have more data and information than ever it is essential to have the knowledge and wisdom to effectively understand and apply it.

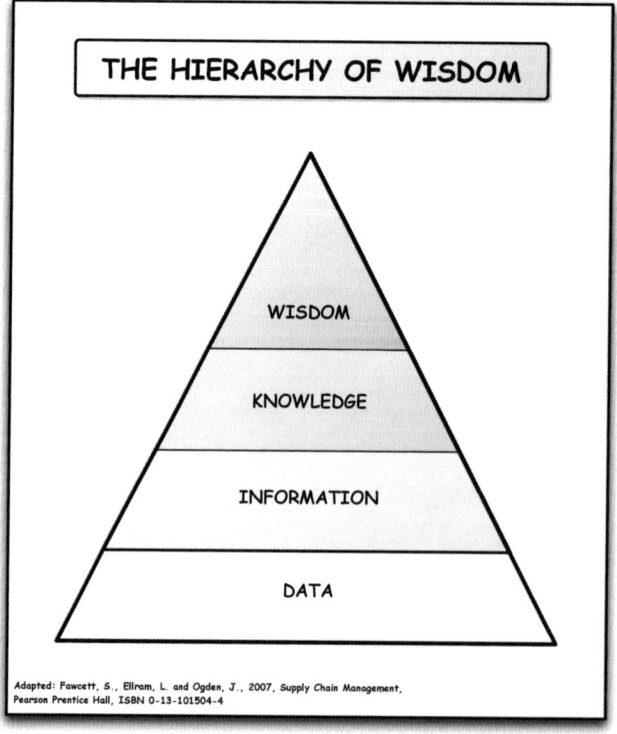

*Figure 1.1.3 - The Hierarchy of Wisdom*

## Differentiation - A New Approach

Just as we live in a world of more data than wisdom, we live in a world where everyone knows the price of everything, but few appreciate value. We are constantly told that what everyone wants is a product or service offering that is:

*good - fast - cheap*

However, if everyone was good, fast and cheap, then, as in some perverse industrial incarnation of Orwell's 1984[10], there would be no differentiation and no choice in the market.

This key concept is illustrated in the "Delight - A Differention Model", (see Figure1.1.4) that describes taking a differentiated position by adjusting the degree of good, fast or cheap, to meet your specific customer's requirements. If your customer requires good and fast then improving these characteristics and being less cheap is a differentiation strategy. If, however, your customer wants cheap and fast they may be happy to pay for more of these qualities even if it is less good. Overall, it is significant to understand the right customer will pay for their preference. Figure 1.1.4 gives examples of points of differentiation in a good-fast-cheap market.

---

[10] George Orwell, *Nineteen Eighty Four,* Secker & Warburg, London, 1949.

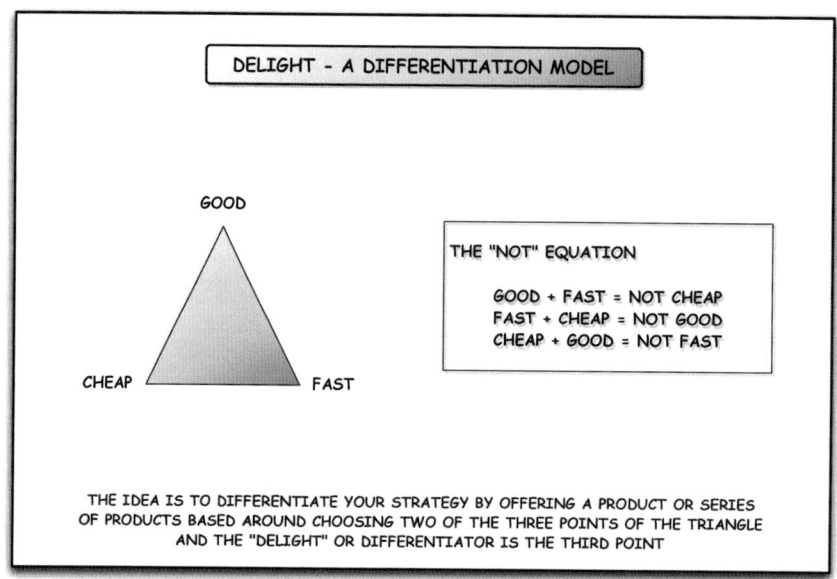

*Figure 1.1.4 - An Example of Points of Differentiation in a Market*

The concept of differentiation and, indeed, breaking down of the axiom regarding good, fast and cheap, is really the first move towards a more sustainable and differentiated strategy for many organisations. The next step is understanding placement of the "stuff we sell".

Figure 1.1.5 provides an illustration of the Opportunity Gauge. The Opportunity Gauge is a quick way to represent that organisations need to target themselves against the right customer base in terms of finding customers who have need for the stuff they sell instead of simply wanting the stuff they sell. Customers are a key focus of a differentiation strategy.

Typically, good spaces can be had from both customer sections, however, in downturn customers who have 'need' will still need to purchase whereas customers who have 'want' may defer that purchase to a later point when times are better, systems improve and/or they have time to shop around. Fundamentally, the concept in terms of differentiation is not only to find that special place, a niche, away from competition within the market place but also to find a position that has a defined customer space where the customer has a definable need for the product or service that is being offered.

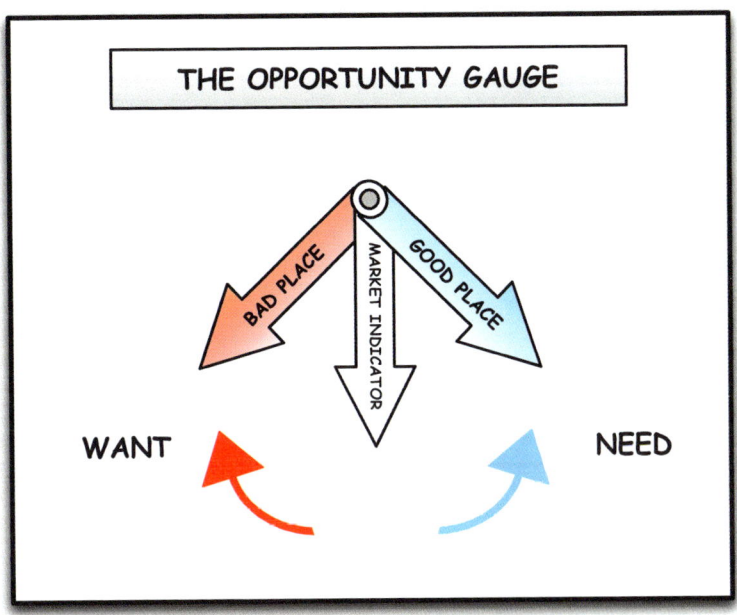

*Figure 1.1.5 - The Opportunity Gauge*

Perhaps the time has come:

*To ask not what it is we do but rather what it is we sell.*

This is a question to keep in mind as you turn to Act 1, Scene 2, which moves on to provide, in their entirety, the original 24 diagnostics that form the initial work and two "bonus" diagnostics that are new to COMPLEXITY.

Act 1, Scene 3, provides some of the feedback and discussions from previous participants of the diagnostics. The past participants have assisted in focusing the work more fully through their feedback and contributions.[11]

Alongside the diagnostics there are a series of good readings and resources and references that back some of the contents or provide counter views to give you the opportunity to further consider the theory that surrounds your own outcomes from the diagnostics and contextualise your findings. I have avoided the more academic sprinkling of references throughout the main works. I have genuinely tried to incorporate all of the main concepts and attribute them back to the authors, however, if you spot something that is missing or inaccurate, I would appreciate feedback to make amends.

*Space: The Final Frontier*
*Success in the free market economy begins with defining*
*what space you are in.*

Scene 2 provides the diagnostic set designed to provide data on where your business is now.

---

[11] The reader is warned that Scene 3 is not for the faint hearted or the traditionalist theorist. This scene offers a somewhat alarming scenario that could be perceived as bleak and treacherous to say the least.

**ACT 1 - SCENE 2**

**EVALUATING WHERE YOUR BUSINESS IS NOW -**

**THE 26 BUSINESS DIAGNOSTICS**

## The Diagnostics

This set of diagnostics has been developed over an industry, private practice and academic career spanning more than 30 years. In response to the positive feedback and significant improvement in measurable business outcomes achieved in industry and private practice, these diagnostics have subsequently been utilised in programs for the Australian Government, within the Sydney Business School as a core within the Executive MBA program and, also successfully deployed in Asia, the Middle East, Indian Subcontinent, Europe and the USA.

The diagnostics have been successfully used in a number of ways, both by individuals and by teams. The recommended approach would be a duality. A business leader might conduct the diagnostics without the deep research or contemplation typically used in the workshop environment, to provide a stake in the ground as to how the leader views the business currently. These results would form the first set of coordinates (points of reference) for evaluating the current position of the business.

Following, or concurrent with the leader's diagnostic evaluation, the same diagnostics conducted in an internal workshop, with team members from different business areas coming together and conducting deeper investigation, would provide a comparison between the leader's perception of the company currently and that of other team members collectively. This combined response would require a sensitive approach and some facilitation in order to develop a rich data set and to remove any potential blame or conflict that might be generated but this approach is highly beneficial in identifying any gaps in perception or understanding of current performance in key areas. The discussion generated in completing these diagnostics is also highly valuable in terms of breaking down silos and identifying issues and opportunities.

*Fundamentally, your organisation is exactly where it is. Its systems have been perfectly designed to give you exactly what you have got.*

The diagnostics identify if a businesses has focused on cost for far too long and, in so doing, lost competitive capability as quality has declined and true overall operating costs have risen. Modern management mantras have too often morphed the wisdom of industry giants; committing businesses to join the stampede of fools to a "get rich quick by cost-cutting" promise that has no foundation and instead commits organisations to a race to the bottom; to the detriment of shareholders, stakeholders, customers, employees and, indeed, future generations.

Sustainability has been reduced, in many cases, to a marketing message to keep customers and the public happy, rather than being a powerful management tool essential for improving core competitive advantage. Similarly, innovation is too often reduced to product specifications rather than being applied to every aspect of the business from organisational structure, role descriptions, renumeration, integration of knowledge, customer collaboration and supplier engagement practices.

These are only two examples of the need to challenge the assumptions that often exist without any awareness and yet constrain business performance and even increase vulnerability and risk in a business environment that is characterised by interdependencies and rapid change.

This first set of diagnostics enables a business to evaluate their current position and find an underlying foundation in order to develop a plan for moving forward. Knowing where you are now is where the focus needs to be, in order to then effectively navigate a way forward to where you want to go.

**Diagnostic 1**

The term b-ecosystem is used to describe a holistic business concept; a big picture perspective of what is really going on in your business both internally and externally. Today a high degree of complex interdependent and interrelated links and processes is experienced by business in many aspects of their operations, including in terms of:

1.  Supply Network Complexity: Most businesses rely on complex networks of suppliers to operate. Outsourcing increases the importance of managing external suppliers and agility demands collaboration with and between suppliers. Many interdependent links are difficult to manage and can increase risk, however, so does dependency on any single supplier.

2.  Process Complexity: Internal and external business processes often have numerous stages with some that need to occur consecutively and others concurrently while all continually complying with changing requirements.

3.  Product Complexity: Products and services become more complex when different materials, volumes, lead times and assemblies are offered and need to respond to changes in demand or design. Product range complexity occurs as variations and new items expand the range offered and elimination of some ranges may be required.

4.  Customer Complexity: Different business requirements and characteristics of each customer, including specific volumes, timing and methods of ordering, increase complexity through the system.

5.  Organisational Complexity: Hierarchical structures of siloed business functions, often with discrete budget targets that engender a short-term, internal efficiency and cost cutting focus rather than an external focus on agility to profitably keep and expand customers and markets, create misalignment of purposes within the organisation.

One of the core concerns of complexity for business management (i.e. the management of the b-ecosystem) is maintaining flow, both in terms of goods and services to the end customer, and revenue and commitment from the end customer.  These principles are well presented in supply chain management theory and practice but typically diluted in the structural silos that often entrap businesses.  The first diagnostic is centered on determining how well you know your supply system and how it is configured.

Diagnostic 1 is a blank sheet of paper that asks the participant to draw the map of their supply chain.  What is required is that all of the inputs into the business are drawn, the value that the business provides is then drawn and the outputs of the business to the customers and the customer's customer and so on, are drawn.  The concept of this particular diagnostic is to set a base line in terms of understanding what the company does and the value that it adds along the whole of the process or within the b-ecosystem.

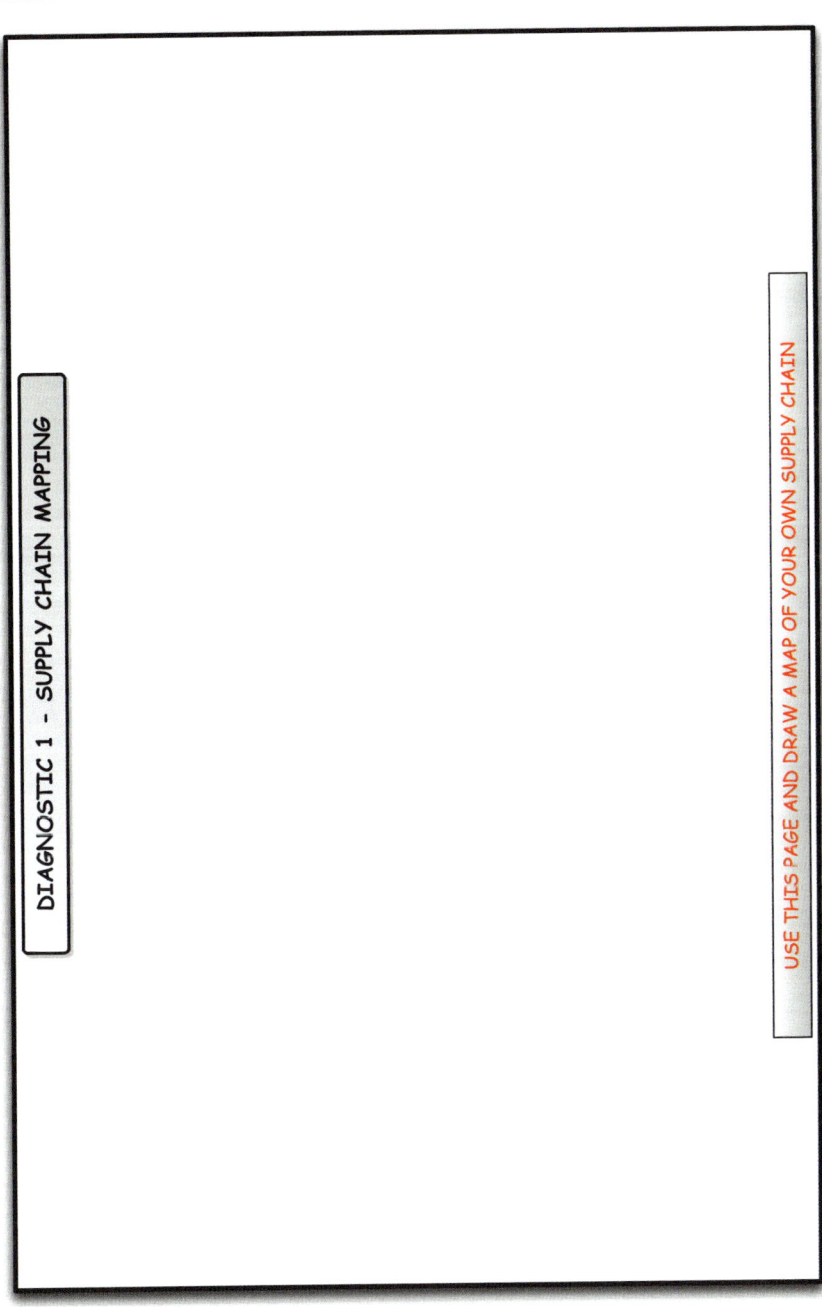

**DIAGNOSTIC 1 - SUPPLY CHAIN MAPPING**

**USE THIS PAGE AND DRAW A MAP OF YOUR OWN SUPPLY CHAIN**

*Diagnostic D1.1 - Mapping the Supply Chain*

## Diagnostic 2

Diagnostic 2 develops an understanding of the risks that could interrupt business, asking you to describe what could happen today to stop your business operating today. These disruptions could be listed as major, medium and minor crises[12] and/or interruptions to flow. This might be through things such as lack of supply of a component or an element of the business, people not turning up to work, major infrastructure outages and so on. Legal and legislative and/or customer demand might also be included within this diagnostic.

---

[12] Crisis is not necessarily a catastrophic event that happens to the business, but rather an unexpected disruption or interruption to the continuity and flow of business activities.

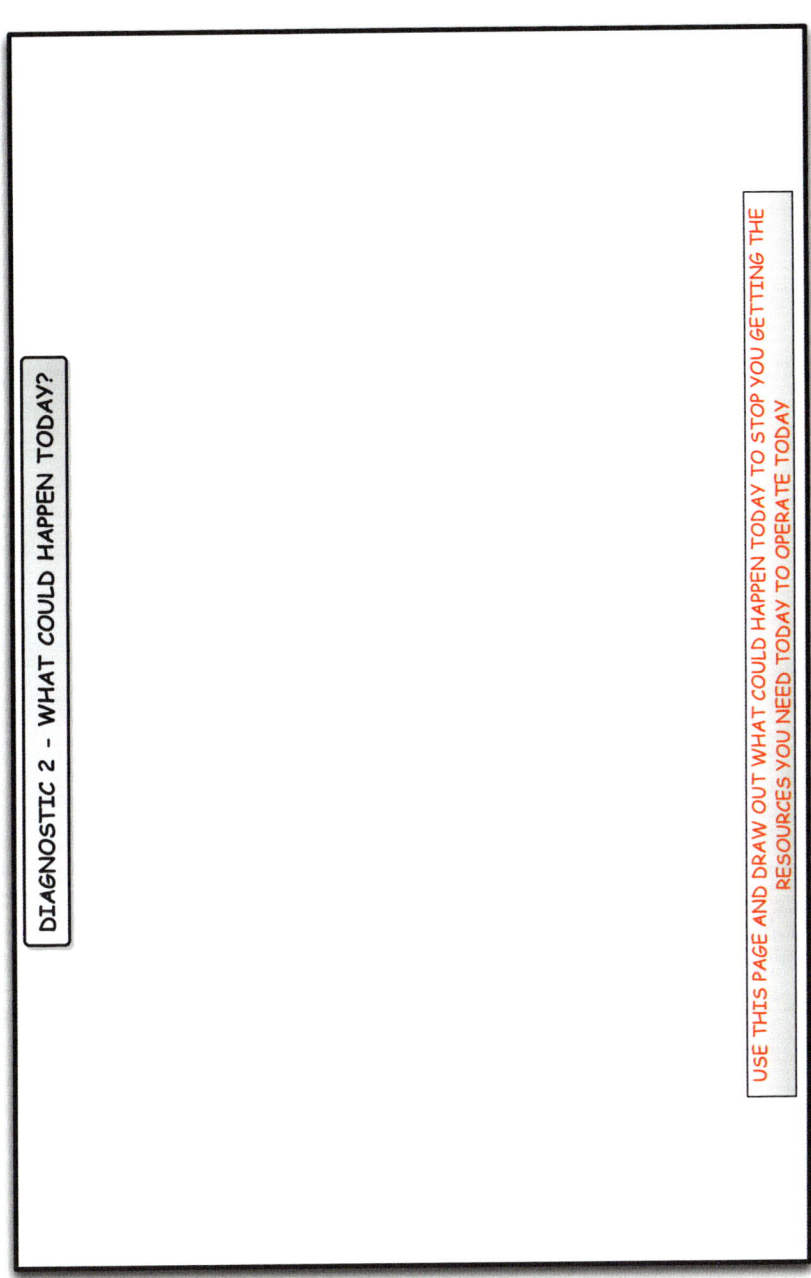

DIAGNOSTIC 2 - WHAT COULD HAPPEN TODAY?

USE THIS PAGE AND DRAW OUT WHAT COULD HAPPEN TODAY TO STOP YOU GETTING THE RESOURCES YOU NEED TODAY TO OPERATE TODAY

*Diagnostic D1.2 - What Could Happen Today to Stop You Operating Today*

## Diagnostic 3

Diagnostic 3 extends the issue of business risk into "futurising" what could happen today that could stop your business getting the resources it needs for tomorrow. Again, things such as unplanned interruption, threats of industrial action, delayed delivery of components or supply, perhaps imported goods being embargoed on the dockside etc, might be considerations within the context of this diagnostic. Political issues and/or changing demand from customers should also be considered.

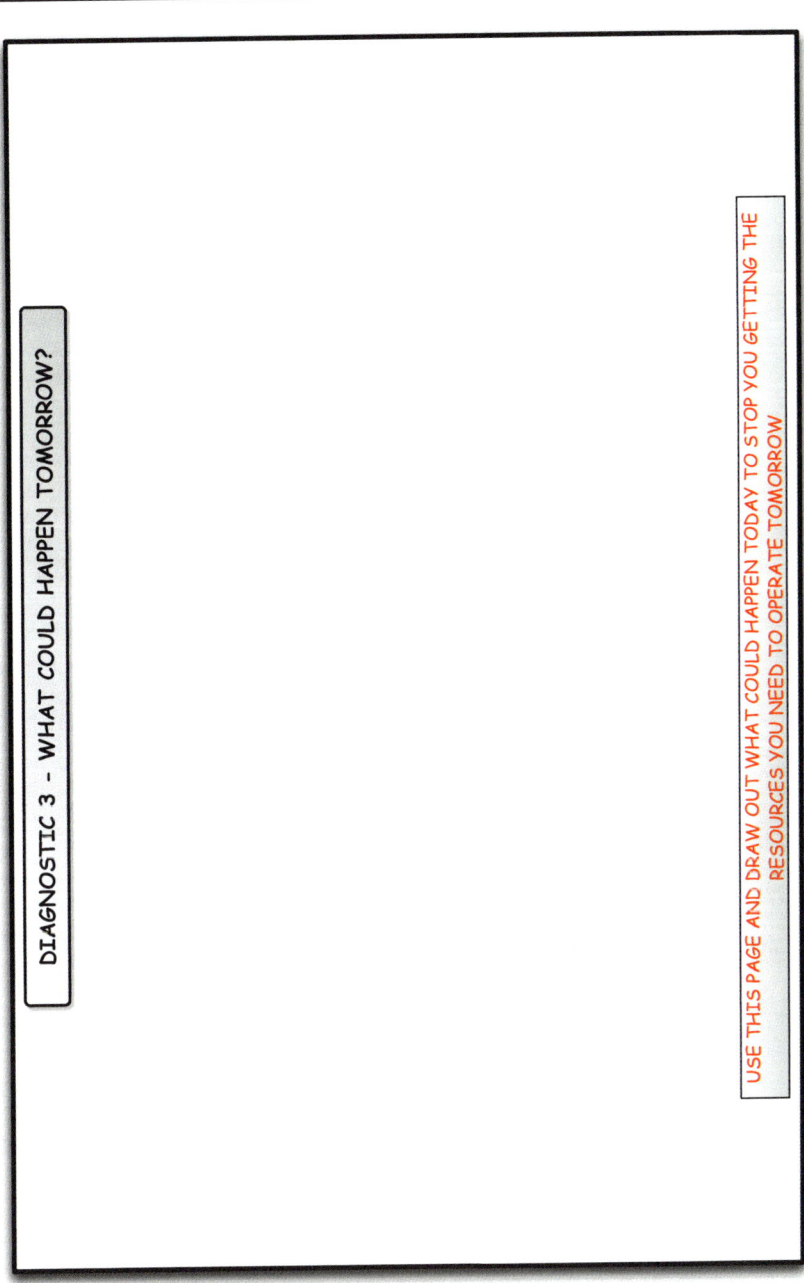

DIAGNOSTIC 3 - WHAT COULD HAPPEN TOMORROW?

USE THIS PAGE AND DRAW OUT WHAT COULD HAPPEN TODAY TO STOP YOU GETTING THE RESOURCES YOU NEED TO OPERATE TOMORROW

*Diagnostic D1.3 - What Could Happen Today to Stop You Operating Tomorrow*

## Diagnostic 4

Diagnostic 4 is a simple risk analysis. There are many good references for risk analysis and ISO Standards for risk analysis. This diagnostic is aimed at business leaders identifying the top five risks that are likely to effect their operation, now and to the mid-term. Experience has shown that depending on the sector, depending on the season and depending on the location these risks can vary exponentially. Risk could be from lack of supply of money to lack of supply of market place, legislative changes, industrial relations, pay scales and even quality or industry standards changing. Fundamentally, by ranking risks 1-5 and looking at the severity of the impact on the organisation and the probability of occurrence, a simple top level risk profile can be generated rapidly. What is also included in this exercise is the opportunity to put some preventative action in place and to list the person who is going to be responsible for putting that action in place. Typically, where there is a risk, the focus of discussion is on whether that risk is going to eventuate or not. This is not the way to approach the question. Rather, although you may not know if the risk is there or going to be there or how big it might be, suppose it happens and consider what the consequences of that would be. Many expensive if not serious mistakes can be prevented by asking, "If this assumption is incorrect, what will be happen?" Often the realisation that fixing a problem will take a lot longer than preventing it, by checking measurements and specifications or proper planning, is a good incentive to make sure things are done properly in the first place. If the consequences of even an unexpected risk would be disastrous, consideration should be given to taking action to mitigate that risk from eventuating or to minimising the consequences if it should occur.

# DIAGNOSTIC 4 – RISK ANALYSIS

## RISK MITIGATION PLAN

| DESCRIPTION OF THE RISK | SEVERITY (1-10) | PROBABILITY (%) | IMPACT ON THE FLOW | PREVENTATIVE ACTION | RESPONSIBLE PERSON |
|---|---|---|---|---|---|
| 1 | | | | | |
| 2 | | | | | |
| 3 | | | | | |
| 4 | | | | | |
| 5 | | | | | |

USE THIS PAGE AND DEVELOP AN ANALYSIS OF THE TOP FIVE RISKS IN YOUR CURRENT SYSTEM

Adapted: Mauch P (2010). Quality Management: Theory and Application

*Diagnostic D1.4 - Risk Mitigation*

## Diagnostic 5

Diagnostic 5 is a SWOT analysis. Although a well known tool, SWOT analysis is typically done extremely badly and the potential of this tool is not realised. Typically, a SWOT analysis will be done as a 2 x 2 matrix (see Figure 1.2.1). In this diagnostic the standard SWOT matrix is not being used but, rather, answers are required for specific questions regarding external threats and opportunities and the internal strengths and weaknesses of the organisation to respond to these external influences.

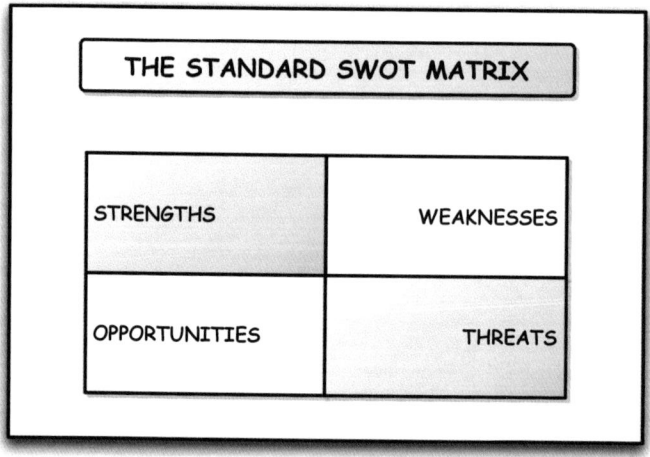

*Figure 1.2.1 - The Standard SWOT Matrix*

This analysis has been designed this way because there is often confusion around terminology, with the quadrant title words potentially having different meanings for participants originating from different social and professional backgrounds. For example, "strengths" could relate to the concepts of "power", "position", "terror", "oppression" or a personal differentiator depending on the participant's personal association with that word. This can lead to a judgmental bias being introduced into the model and, as such, leads to deviation from the standard analysis and/or contributes to a distorted perspective being derived from the application of the model that, in turn, provides ambiguous or meaningless results.

Furthermore, there is often simply not enough detail put into models such as SWOT and, more often than not, the depth of the analysis is poor. The SWOT analysis as part of this diagnostic, has been developed from an original MindMap by Buzan (See Figure 1.2.2) and it has further been converted into a table that asks basic questions in each of the 4 categories of SWOT.

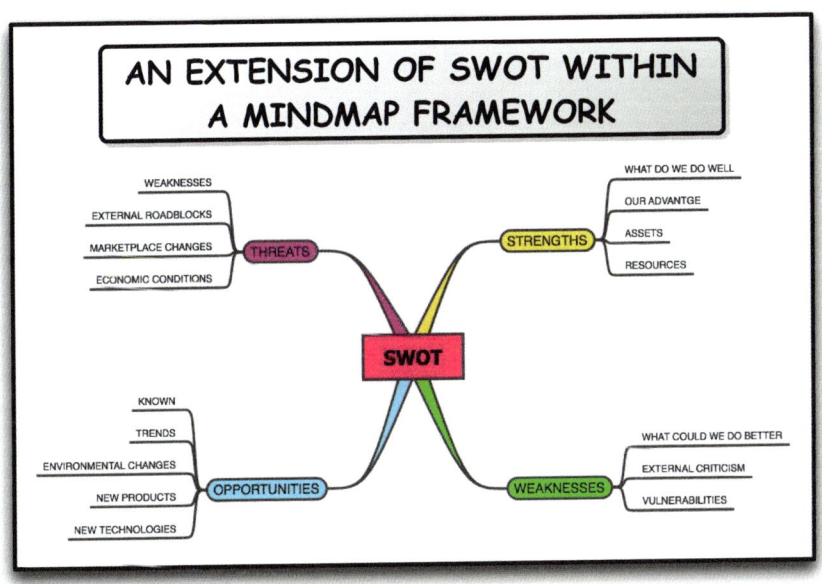

(MindMap adapted Buzan 2005)

*Figure 1.2.2 - An Extension of SWOT Within a MindMap Framework*

The benefit of the table approach is that, instead of trying to interpret what 'strengths' means for example, the participant is now asked a series of direct questions that need to be addressed in detail. For example, instead of being asked "What is your strength?", you are being asked "What does your business do well?" "What is your advantage?" "What assets do you have?" "What resources can you call upon?" By answering the questions directly, a much more detailed picture is delivered around a company's characteristics and capabilities.

## DIAGNOSTIC 5 - EXTENDED SWOT ANALYSIS

| THE EXTENDED SWOT ANALYSIS | | |
|---|---|---|
| EXTERNAL OPPORTUNITIES | WHAT DO WE KNOW IS OUT THERE | |
| | WHAT ARE THE TRENDS | |
| | WHAT ARE THE ENVIRONMENTAL CHANGES | |
| | WHAT NEW PRODUCT WOULD THE MARKET WELCOME | |
| | WHAT TECHNOLOGIES COULD CHALLENGE OUR POSITION | |
| EXTERNAL THREATS | WHERE ARE WE WEAK | |
| | WHAT EXTERNAL ROADBLOCKS EXIST | |
| | WHAT MARKETPLACE CHANGES HAVE TAKEN PLACE RECENTLY | |
| | WHAT ARE THE CURRENT ECONOMIC CONDITIONS | |
| INTERNAL STRENGTHS | WHAT DO WE DO WELL | |
| | WHAT IS OUR ADVANTAGE | |
| | WHAT ARE OUR ASSETS | |
| | WHAT ARE OUR RESOURCES | |
| INTERNAL WEAKNESSES | WHAT COULD WE DO BETTER | |
| | WHAT EXTERNAL CRITICISM IS THERE | |
| | WHAT ARE OUR VULNERABILITIES | |

USE THIS PAGE AND DEVELOP A SWOT ANALYSIS OF YOUR BUSINESS - NOTE THE CONTEXTUAL REFERENCE IN TERMS OF "EXTERNAL" AND "INTERNAL" VIEWS

*Diagnostic D1.5 - Extended SWOT Analysis*

## Diagnostic 6

Diagnostic 6 is based around the context of winning or being superior in the operational area that the organisation contests. This diagnostic is split into two main areas: threshold capabilities and capabilities for competitive advantage. Importantly, the diagnostic considers both the tangible and intangible aspects of the organisation from a resource point of view and the tangible and intangible aspects of the organisation from a competencies point of view. A tangible resource may be an advanced production facility. An intangible resource may be a trademark. Tangible competencies are often specific to a business and developed over time, such as a highly efficient production systems. Intangible competencies might be a business culture of innovation, a reputation for inventiveness or great team work.

There are many theoretical concepts that talk about "threshold capabilities". Fundamentally, threshold capabilities are what an organisation needs just to participate within any given sector (i.e. have skin in the game). These capabilities might be legislative, they might be around licensing, or skills and/or knowledge acquisition. Competitive advantage is not derived from the threshold capabilities but, rather, from competencies that have developed that provide something extra; a "uniqueness" or point of differentiation or added value. Particularly if a competency is hard to imitate or costly to replicate, it can give an organisation the edge. These competitive advantage capabilities are things above and beyond the threshold, the things that are going to make the difference and provide the initial differentiator and agent for change; the things that determine why your customers buy from you and what your business does to delight your customer.

**DIAGNOSTIC 6 – ASSETS TO WIN YOUR SPACE**

RESOURCES NECESSARY FOR WINNING IN YOUR SPACE

| | RESOURCES | | COMPETENCIES | |
| --- | --- | --- | --- | --- |
| | TANGIBLE | INTANGIBLE | TANGIBLE | INTANGIBLE |
| CAPABILITIES (WHAT YOU NEED JUST TO BE IN THE GAME) | | | | |
| CAPABILITIES FOR COMPETITIVE ADVANTAGE (WHAT YOU NEED TO WIN) | | | | |

USE THIS PAGE AND AND NOTE THE BASIC CAPABILITIES YOU NEED TO BE IN THE SPACE YOU ARE IN AND THE EXTRA CAPABILITIES NEEDED TO BE COMPETITIVE

*Diagnostic D1.6 - Assets Needed to Win In Your Chosen Contested Market (Space)*

## Diagnostic 7

Diagnostic 7 is Porter's Five Forces Model (Porter 1980) (see Figure 1.2.3). This is a powerful tool when used correctly and, contextually, it provides a complementary stance to the other diagnostics.

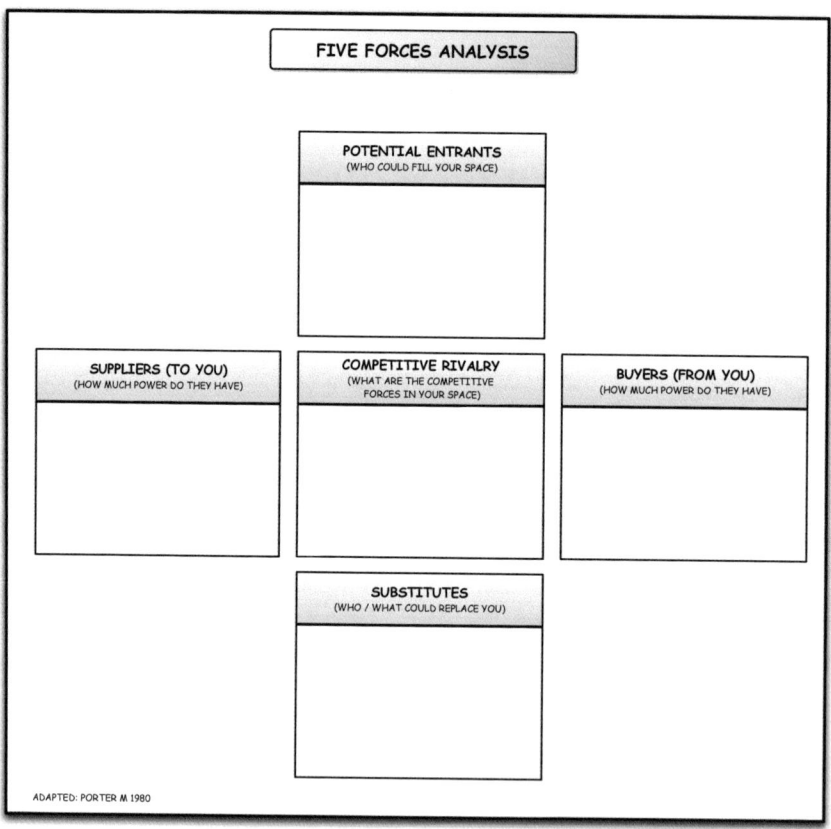

*Figure 1.2.3 - Porters Five Forces Model*

Very simply, Porter argued that profitability is driven by the competitive intensity that comes from the five competitive forces identified in the model. The model shows that competitive forces extend beyond direct competition from your business rivals. The model provides a broader perspective for considering competitive advantage by assessing the competitive forces within the industry. The five forces considered are: the potential for new entrants to move into your contested market space; the power suppliers have over your business; the power buyers have over your business; the substitutes and internal rivalry that could impact on your business and, of course, the competition from your rivals contesting the same market space. The model enables your organisation to consider these forces and the way these forces interact to shape the competitive advantage your business can establish.

The model is included in these diagnostics to develop insights into how your business might begin to think about differentiation within the space or area of your operations. It is recommended that participants begin by filling the centre section concerning rivalry from your business competitors and describe or list what's going on in their particular part of your market or industry.[13] From there, it is possible to determine the main factors that impact on your business from the other four segments.

[13] This diagnostic has therefore been designed accordingly.

| DIAGNOSTIC 7 - FIVE FORCES ANALYSIS | |
|---|---|
| COMPETITIVE RIVALRY | WHAT ARE THE COMPETITIVE FORCES IN YOUR SPACE? |
| BUYERS (FROM YOU) | HOW MUCH POWER DO THEY HAVE? |
| SUPPLIERS (TO YOU) | HOW MUCH POWER DO THEY HAVE? |
| POTENTIAL ENTRANTS & SUBSTITUTES | WHO COULD FILL YOUR SPACE? |
| SUBSTITUTES & INTERNAL RIVALRY | WHAT ARE THE COMPETITIVE FORCES IN YOUR SPACE? |

ADAPTED: PORTER M 1980

*Diagnostic D1.7 - Five Forces Analysis*

## Diagnostic 8

"Analysis paralysis" describes a situation of spending so much time internally analysing a situation that we can't make decisions and become ineffective in terms of our ability to see or move towards a future goal. To avoid analysis paralysis an alternative concept of an "over-the-horizon" strategy and/or "future seeing" is based on the notion that if you stood on the sea shore, looking out to sea, the furthest you could see would be to the horizon. What would happen, or what advantage would you gain if, for example, you could be higher than anybody else around you and effectively see further to your own "new horizon"? Take that one step further and what would happen if you had the capability to see over the horizon and view things coming well before anybody else?

Diagnostic 8 offers a first stage opportunity to describe what the future looks like in the long term for your organisation. For example, what could the market trends be? Who might the key players be? What customer demand is there likely to be and/or what market segments are likely to develop into the longer term? Importantly, this diagnostic asks you to consider the future not according to what you might want it to be but according to what you might expect it to be, based on what you know now.

**DIAGNOSTIC 8 - OVER THE HORIZON / FUTURE SEEING THE ORGANISATION**

*Diagnostic D1.8 - Over the Horizon / Future Seeing the Organisation*

## Diagnostic 9

At this point, participants are encouraged to think about their overall supply network and/or operational flow once again (i.e. their b-ecosystem). Taking into account the seven diagnostics that have been completed and viewing the original supply chain map, you are asked to redraw your supply network, considering it against your answers to the diagnostics so far.

It should be noted that although you are asked to complete this diagnostic now in relation to the previous diagnostics, it is also recommended that you return to this particular diagnostic again, once you have read Act 2 (particularly Scenes 3, 4 and 5).[14] At this point, participants often begin to see a much more complex and also much more varied map emerge and they typically begin to think about the tangible and intangible resources and knowledge necessary to perform the core functions of the business and also to think about the future opportunities within a market place etc.

---

[14] With this in mind, diagnostic 9 had been repeated in this section as D1.9.1 to be completed post the completion of Act 2in the second book in the trilogy.

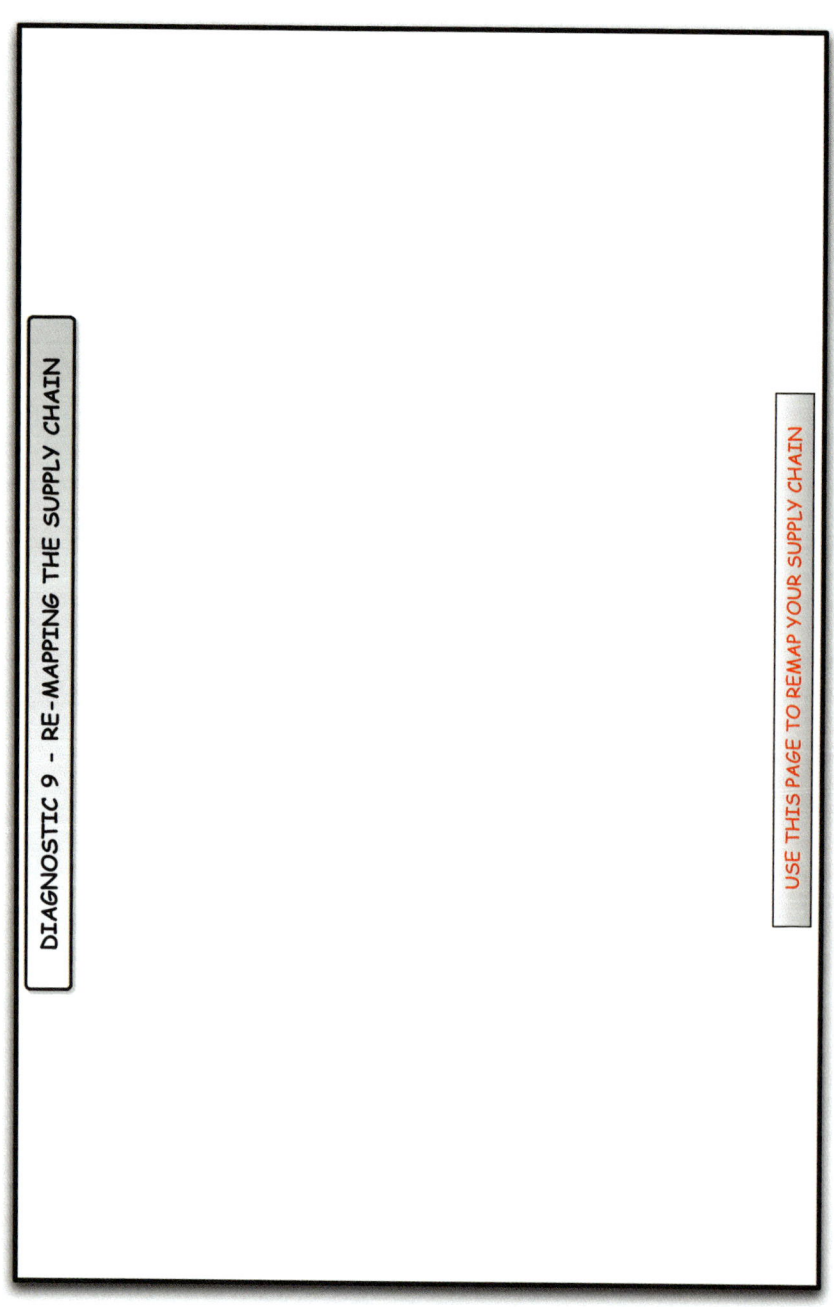

DIAGNOSTIC 9 - RE-MAPPING THE SUPPLY CHAIN

USE THIS PAGE TO REMAP YOUR SUPPLY CHAIN

*Diagnostic D1.9 - Re-mapping the Supply Chain*

DIAGNOSTIC 9.1 - RE-MAPPING THE BUSINESS SYSTEM POST COMPLETION OF ACT 2

USE THIS PAGE TO REMAP YOUR BUSINESS SYSTEM POST COMPLETION OF ACT 2 SHOWING KEY NODAL LINKS AND INTERACTIONS

*Diagnostic D1.9.1 - Re-mapping the Supply Chain (Business System) -*
*Post Completion of Act 2*

## Diagnostic 10

Diagnostic 10 is in two parts and it begins to extend the view of the business. The first part of this diagnostic talks about finding a "happy place" for the organisation, effectively a pivotal or central role between your business activities and those of your customers and suppliers, as illustrated in Figure 1.2.4. What is the happy place or the 'edge' that your organisation provides?

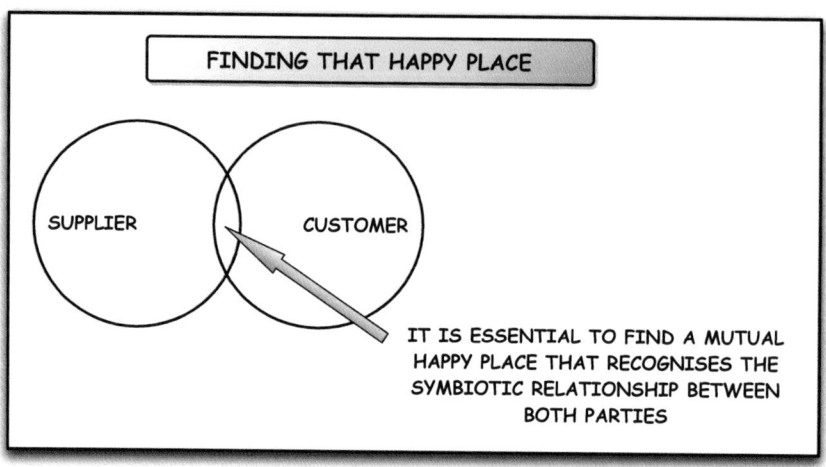

*Figure 1.2.4 - The Mutual Relationship Between Players in the Business Ecosystem*

The second part of this diagnostic centres on finding the central point within a market. This requires consideration of whether there is truly a market that has tangible and viable customers, whether it is realistic for your business to enter this market and establish lasting business and whether, situationally, your organisation is ready and prepared to take that position or needs to take that position and if there are any other circumstances for your business that drive or stop you from competing in that market (see Figure 1.2.5). This is the crux of business competitiveness and separates the "should do" from the "can do" or a dream from a competitive competence.

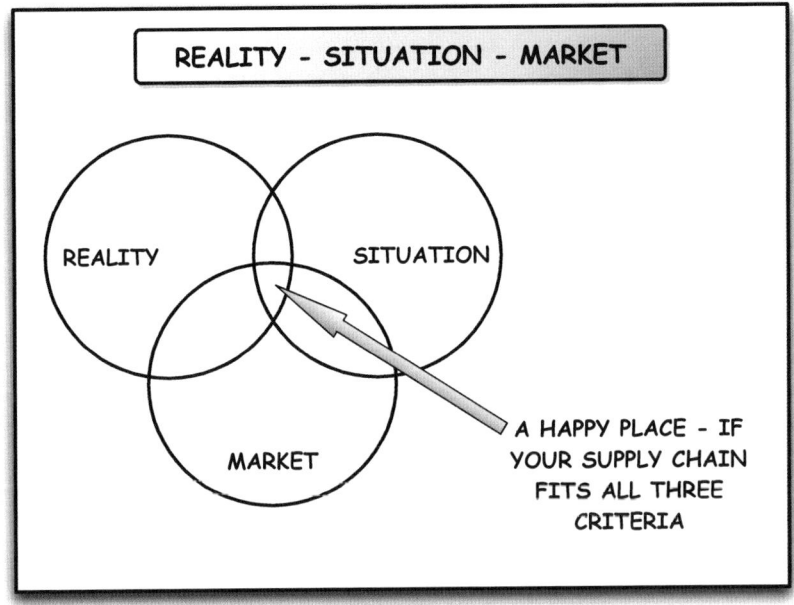

*Figure 1.2.5 - Alignment and Triangulation of Business Dynamics*

Diagnostic 10 in many ways begins the heartfelt search that starts to determine whether an organisation has the capability to be competitive into the long term. In many respects, this is one of the hardest diagnostics for participants to complete because, whereas on the one hand they want to say that everything they are doing does have a relatively real situational context, more often than not, much of the analysis is based on dreams or assumptions, both of which are dangerous and on the margins of reality without understanding of the fundamental business dynamics, i.e. the realities of the business (see Figure 1.2.6 and a modified interpretation of Taguchi's Economic View).

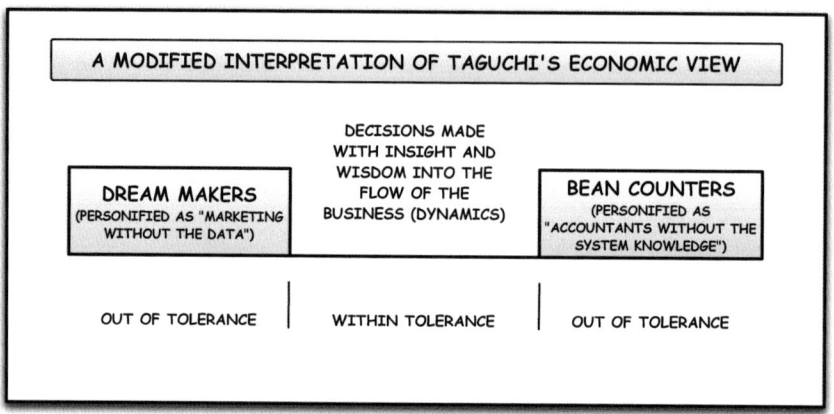

*Figure 1.2.6 - "Dream Makers and Bean Counters -*
*On the Margins of the Reality of Business Dynamics - A modified*
*Interpretation of Taguchi's Economic View*

Genichi Taguchi's basic principle suggested a boundary condition was established where anything produced within the boundary was considered to be of good quality or merchantable quality (i.e. in tolerance) and anything produced outside of the boundary was considered to be out of tolerance and therefore wasteful. This modified interpretation of Taguchi is that dream makers, for example, represent the situation or proposition in a distorted or misinformed manner and are therefore out of tolerance (or perhaps should not be tolerated). The other boundary is represented by "bean counters", not to be mistaken with accountants but rather anyone who processes raw data without understanding or often caring how the system works and, once again, are out of tolerance with their assumptions and decisions.

| DIAGNOSTIC 10 - STRATEGIC FIT | |
|---|---|
| THE MUTUAL HAPPY SPACE | WHAT IS YOUR CENTRAL POINT IN YOUR BUSINESS ECOSYSTEM |
| | |
| THE ECOSYSTEM HAPPY SPACE | IS YOUR ECOSYSTEM REAL - WHY? |
| | |
| | IS YOUR ECOSYSTEM POSITIONED IN THE RIGHT SITUATIONAL CONTEXT - HOW? |
| | |
| | DOES YOUR ECOSYSTEM HAVE A CONTESTABLE MARKET - HOW & WHY |
| | |

*Diagnostic D1.10 - Consideration of Strategic Fit*

## Diagnostic 11

Diagnostic 11 expands on the dream verses reality concept further and was actually a statement by Dr Dan Park. Dan, a global economist, consults to organisations around the world and came up with his principle of "economics 101", which, and I "Couldn't have said it better", states:

> *"For any organisation to survive they fundamentally need to find customers who have both the demand and the ability to pay."*

Diagnostic 11 requires the participant to list those companies that have demand but don't pay and those customers that have demand and do pay.

Fundamentally, those that have the demand and pay are those who form the nucleus of any future longevity for a business and are also those who are likely to set or direct future strategy.

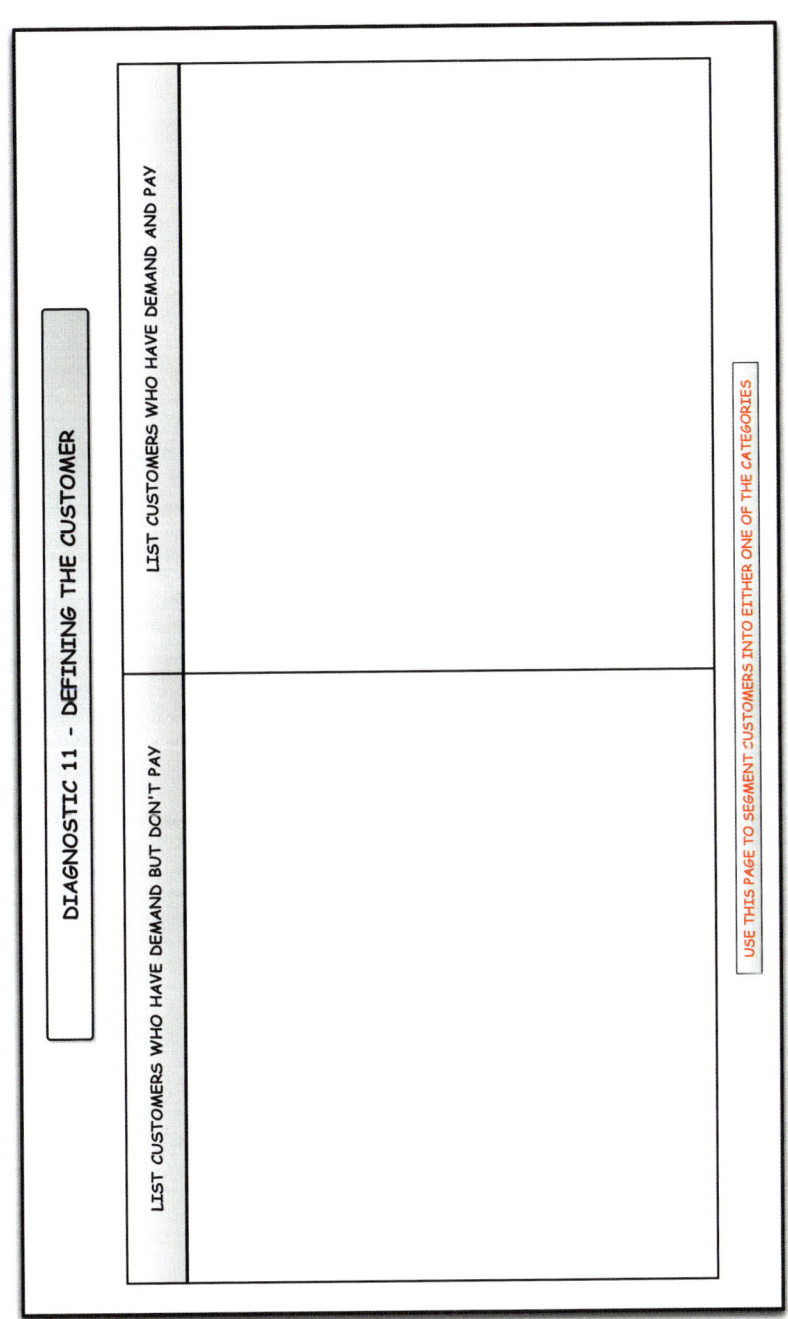

*Diagnostic D1.11 - Defining the Customer*

**Diagnostic 12**

Diagnostic 12 asks three fundamental questions of the leadership of your organisation. The first question is how operational costs are managed, contained and, in some cases, reduced. The next question is how stakeholder or shareholder value is managed and, in many cases, increased. Finally, the third question is how your business manages, maintains and improves its time-to-market. In this case, the diagnostic should be considered almost as a compliance test, with clear statements and evidence provided to back up those statements.

Time-to-market has somehow been relegated to an initiative that was "so last century", but in real terms it demanded more efficacy than the current calls for innovation and there was a tangible measure and benchmark capability. Time-to-market principles offer a significant opportunity to differentiate in terms of market (space) control and customer focus (this is discussed further in Act 2). Cost management is a clear and present necessity and at no point is cost management discounted in this work. However:

*You cannot save your way to success.*

As such, cost savings via, for example, operational improvements, should not be passed onto the customer as a price down incentive when operating in a differentiated market.

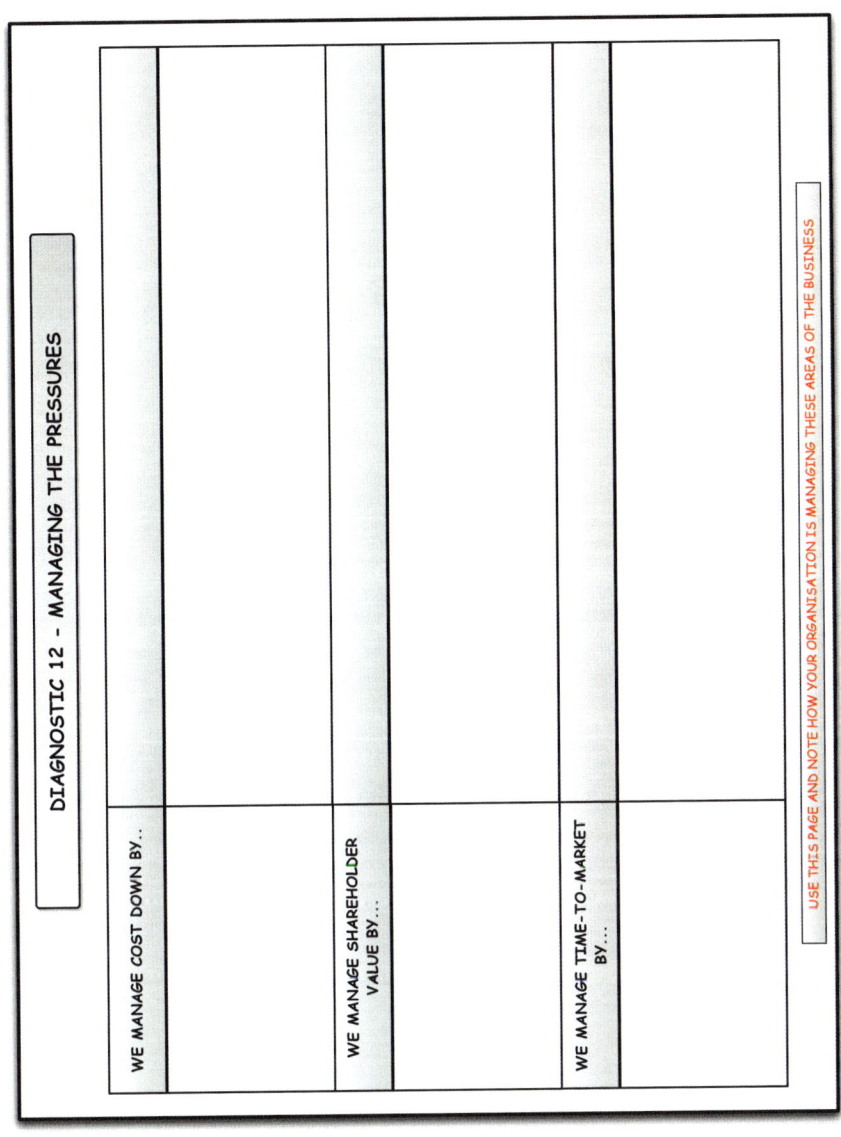

DIAGNOSTIC 12 - MANAGING THE PRESSURES

WE MANAGE COST DOWN BY...

WE MANAGE SHAREHOLDER VALUE BY...

WE MANAGE TIME-TO-MARKET BY...

USE THIS PAGE AND NOTE HOW YOUR ORGANISATION IS MANAGING THESE AREAS OF THE BUSINESS

*Diagnostic D1.12 - Managing the Pressures*

## Diagnostic 13

Innovation is one of the current management buzz words. It seems that wherever you turn, "what every company wants is more innovation", however, there is never a clear statement in terms of how that innovation is going to occur within any given organisational situation or, indeed, what precisely innovation is. We seem to have lost the connection between innovation and invention and, importantly, invention and product development. Diagnostic 13 asks you to identify your current strategy on new product releases.

Recently, the gap between innovation, invention and product development seems to have widened, particularly in the case of businesses where "e" has morphed to the point that it almost stands for "everything" (i.e. the only business you can now have is an "e" businesses). Business leaders have somehow become hypnotised by the concept of "e" and associated social media, almost as the only way out of their predicaments and almost as they have done before with tulip bulbs and spices. However basic laws of commerce and business must still apply in an "e" business as they do within a traditional business. This is illustrated in Figure 1.2.7.

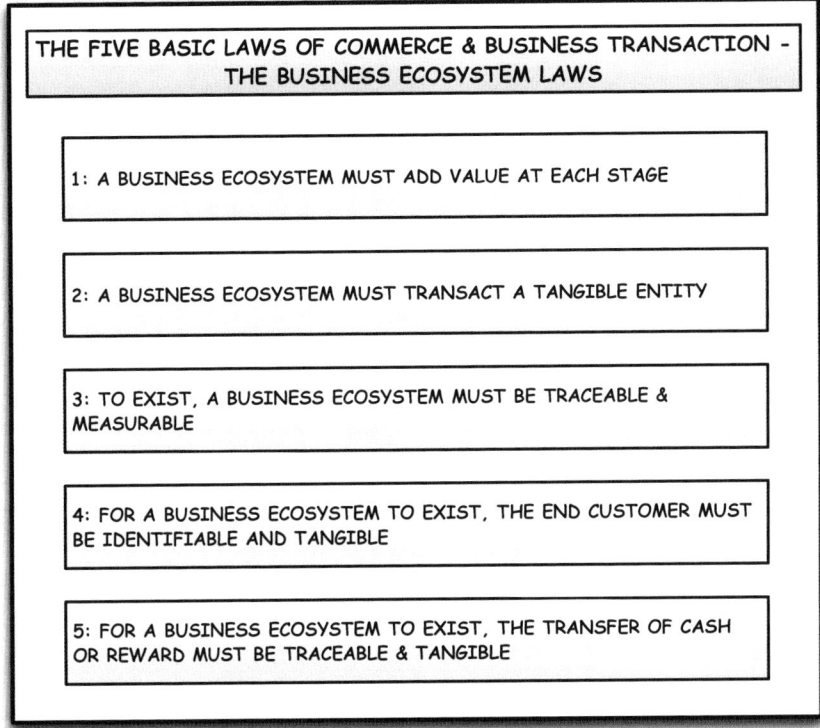

*Figure 1.2.7 - The Five Basic Laws of Commerce and Business Transaction*

Put simply:

*Business cannot live on clicks alone.*

In the next book in this series, the process of product platforming, new product development, issues of time-to-market and the ability to control a market place and remain competitive through new product development will be discussed. In the context of Diagnostic 13, however, the idea is to begin to map how current and future product iterations can be used competitively within the market place. Put simply, you are asked to describe what your new product roll-out strategy is, how and when you execute it and what is the timing of each new product entering the market.

A product platform refers to a base product that can be augmented or "bettered" with small changes that do not alter the base architecture of the platform, for example, a plain hamburger may be the platform from which a version with lettuce is offered, then later another version with lettuce and tomato. The product platform allows you to differentiate your product to delight your customers but without requiring high additional costs to change design or methods of production.

DIAGNOSTIC 13 - PRODUCT STRATEGY, ROLL OUT & PLATFORMS

USE THIS PAGE TO DRAW OUT THE PRODUCT STRATEGY FOR YOUR ORGANISATION

*Diagnostic D1.13 - Setting Product Strategy*

**Diagnostic 14**

Diagnostic 14 follows a similar principle to Diagnostic 13 in continuing the consideration of strategic differentiation within a market place. Differentiating you own organisation is one thing and it is dependent on many variables, including your current customer dynamic, size and market locations, etc. (see Figure 1.2.8). What seldom seems to happen within a differentiation strategy or a differentiation exercise, however, is for organisations to map their own intent against that of their suppliers or, indeed, their customers.

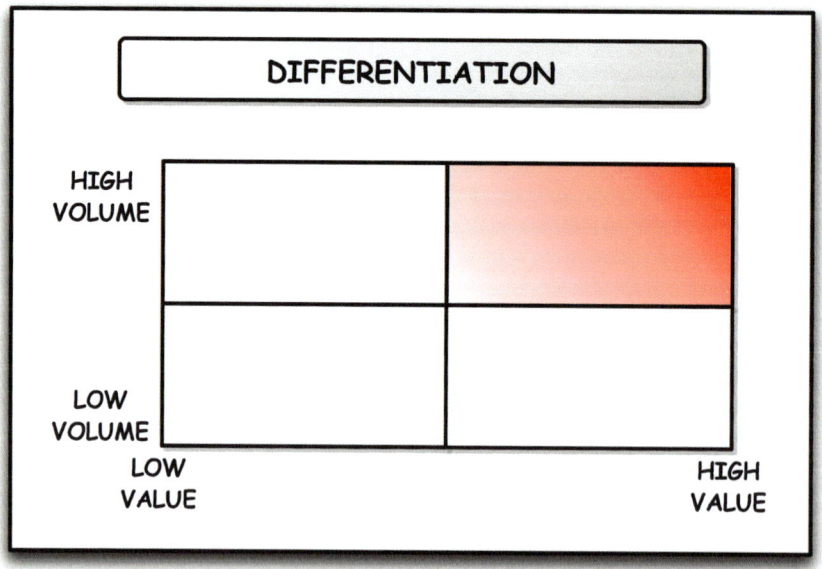

*Figure 1.2.8 - The Concept of Differentiation*

Theoretically, putting a mark on the correct quadrant is easy and often provides a feel good for leaders but some important dynamics must be considered that have significant bearing on the entire competitive construct of the business.

Firstly, the top righthand quadrant (i.e. high volume and high value) is a management mirage. It simply does not exist in the applied business world. The more volume the organisation generates the less value is created. As such, the ratio of the quadrants changes in relation to volume and value perceptions (see Figure 1.2.9).

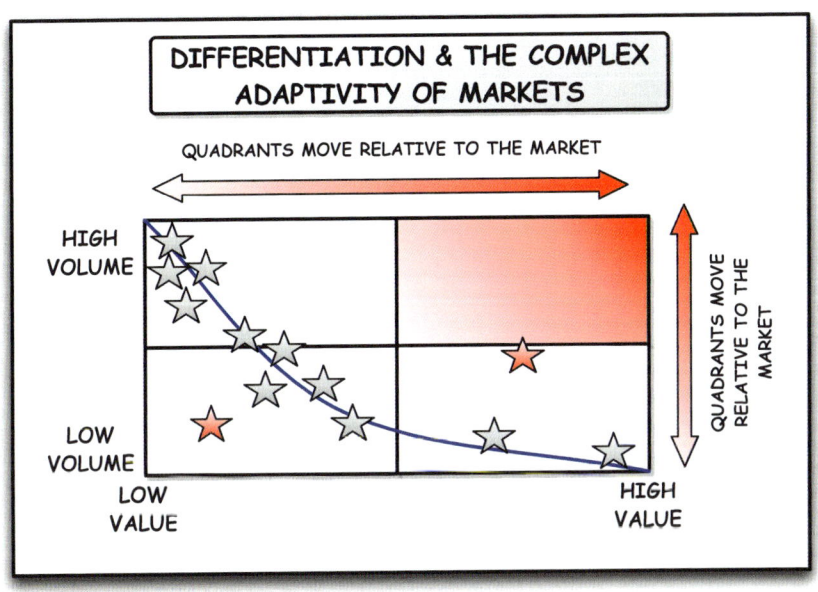

*Figure 1.2.9 - Differentiation and The Complex Adaptivity of Markets*

Typically, in any given market, organisations spread out along a distribution curve and contest entrenched and well defended positions. In their fight to gain even modest percentage growths, they lose sight of the outliers and often discount them as inconsequential players.

Outliers are organisations that generate great businesses in areas of the market that are nearly uncontested. These are the businesses that effectively push the boundaries of the quadrants, to deliver maximum volume at maximum value or minimal volume at minimal value; for example self-published books that might sell slowly but as print-on-demand items can remain available for a much longer period of time than traditionally published and distributed books and, therefore, can provide a viable return in the long run, particularly if the author is continuing to put a range of different books in the market so that while each may sell comparatively few volumes the combined total provides an acceptable income. Outlier businesses are, typically, the "category killer" businesses that change paradigms and the overall balance of power in a heavily contested market.

**Decision Making for Defining Your Differentiated Space**

During any change (transition planned or crisis un-planned) organisations often forget that it is the whole b-ecosystem that has to change. For example, an organisation focused on volume and throughput will be designed to operate within a completely different b-ecosystem to one focused on value and scarcity (see Figure 1.2.10).

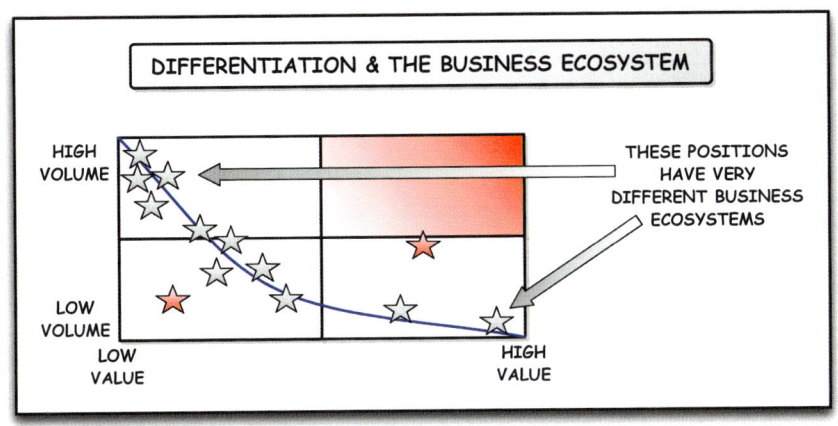

*Figure 1.2.10 - Differentiation and The Business Ecosystem*

This is perhaps the tyranny of management education and the concept that one-size-fits-all. Whereas it is easy to teach and consult within this one-size-fits-all paradigm, it is impossible to apply a one-size-fits-all strategy within a differentiated market and generate a robust stance in the chosen space. Put simply, businesses are b-ecosystems and, as such, a clear understanding of the unique b-ecosystem of each business is required. Any change made without first understanding the b-ecosystem is likely to cause damage. Unfortunately, much business teaching and consulting relies on simple, one dimensional modeling (i.e. basic SWOT) to overcome complex multi-dimensional challenges. By viewing the business within the context of a b-ecosystem, it is possible to drive decision making through applied data (see Figure 1.2.11).

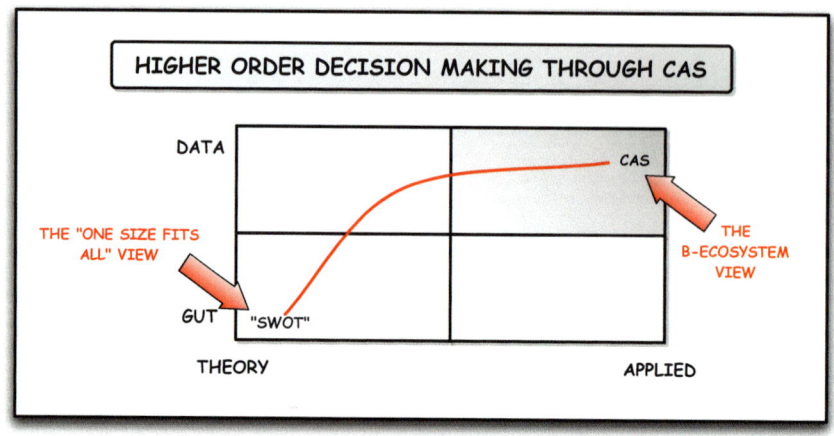

*Figure 1.2.11 - Viewing the Business with a Complex Adaptive System (CAS) Perspective Driving Applied Data Decision Making*

Figure 1.2.11 illustrates that theory, observation and expectation is one level of decision making but greater understanding is achieved through adding data and applying knowledge and testing. This greater understanding becomes increasingly necessary for making strategic differentiation decisions as complexity increases. Diagnostic 14 provides an opportunity to map where your organisation is strategically positioned in the market. This diagnostic asks, in terms of volume and value, where are you and where are your competitors? Is your business, for example, a high volume, low cost provider, or a low volume, high value provider etc. What is your largest competitor? Where are your other competitors? Clearly, the idea is to do a gap analysis between your own differentiation and theirs.

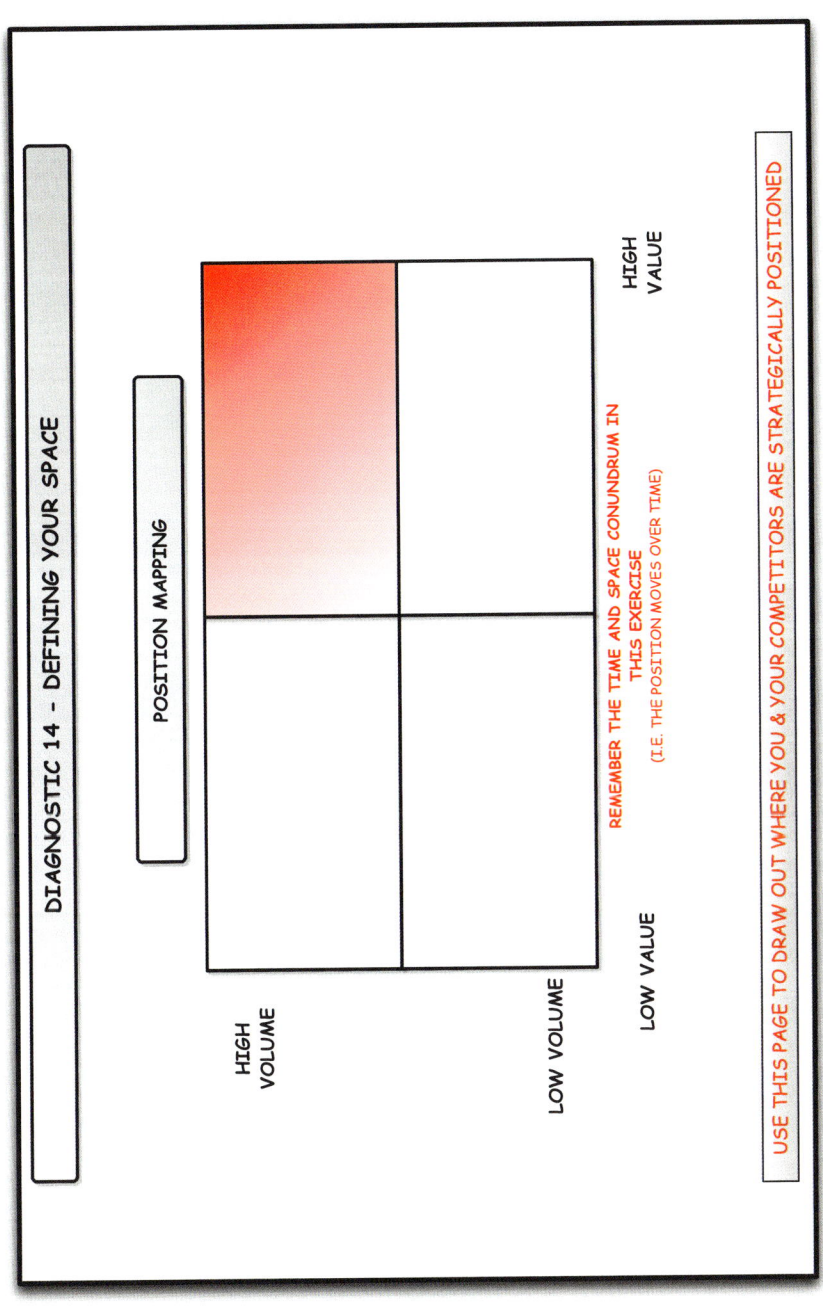

*Diagnostic D1.14 - Defining Strategic Positions*

## Diagnostic 15

Diagnostic 15 is also a mapping and gap analysis exercise but, in this case, it maps suppliers and customers against the same criteria. The triangulation of mapping is critical because an organisation might, for example, be a high value niche player but if its customers are typically looking for a volume or a cost solution they are unlikely to be a customer for long, unless the organisation can move itself into that position. In this context, the triangulation of strategic positioning (i.e. the differentiation characteristics of your organisation, your suppliers and your customers) provides the gap analysis for future strategy.

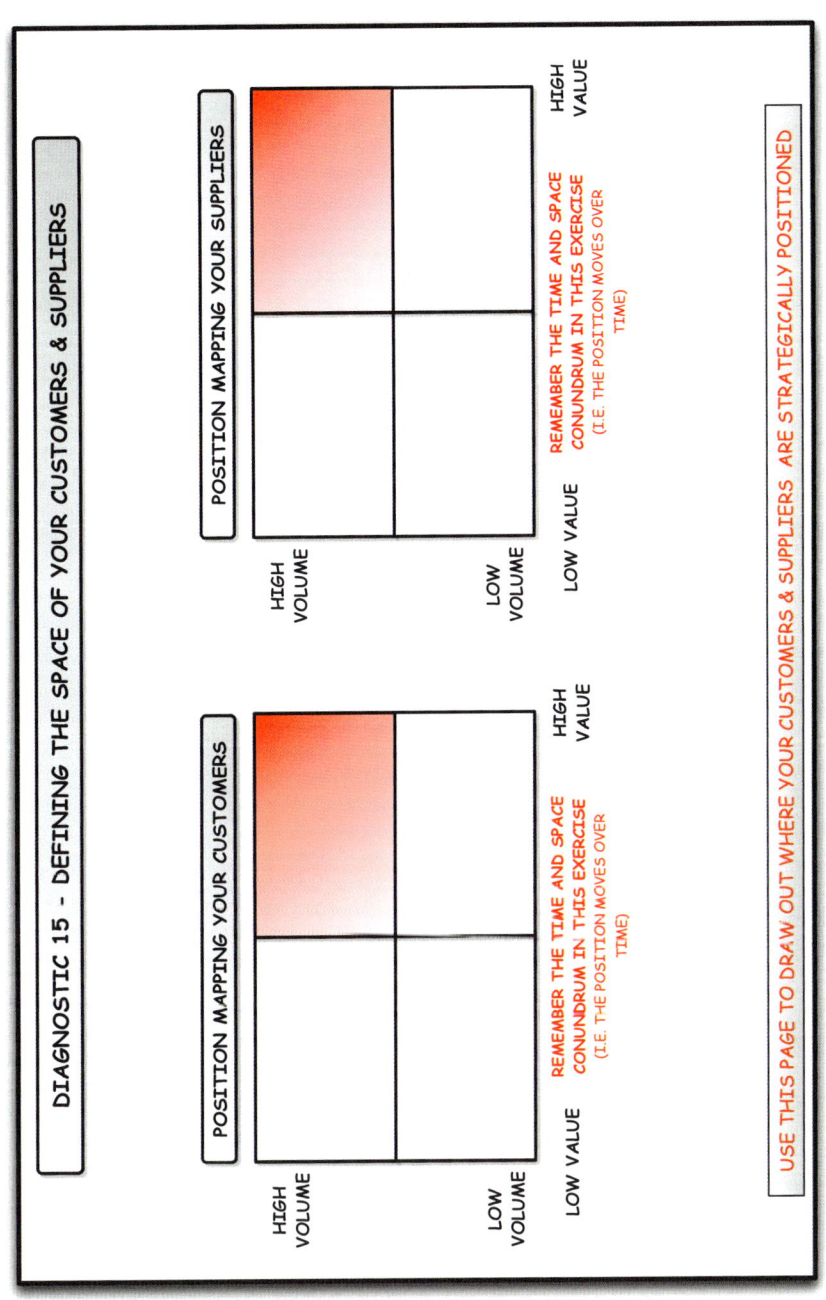

*Diagnostic D1.15 - Defining Your Customer and Supplier Positions*

## Diagnostic 16

Diagnostic 16 brings the last three diagnostics together to provide a sketch of a strategic plan moving forward. From the evaluation of your business based on the previous diagnostics, it should be possible to develop a sketch for how your organisation could move forward in terms of innovation or product strategy, supplier strategy and positioning, customer positioning and strategy and where you move in these areas. These are some important determinants in how successfully you are going to transition your business from A (where it is now) to B (where you want or need it to go).

DIAGNOSTIC 16 - REDEFINING YOUR SPACE

USE THIS PAGE TO MAP HOW YOU MOVE FROM WHERE YOU ARE TO WHERE YOU NEED TO BE

*Diagnostic D1.16 - Redefining Your Space*

## Diagnostic 17

"Marketing triggers demand, sales trigger supply". Within a business context, the concept of sales is typically well understood but not necessarily always that well manifest. In business education, sales is treated almost as a dirty cousin and coverage is limited, if not non-existent. This has significant implications. Sales is a critical business activity. All businesses understand sales; even if they are not very good at it. All businesses that have longevity know they have to sell. However, in business education, sales is typically not covered at all and, where it is covered, it is positively remedial in most cases leading to a false impression on the "leaders of tomorrow" that sales is an unnecessary "waste" and marketing, when done well "is all that is needed" (i.e. a passive interaction with the end customer). Indeed, there is evidence dating back to the 1980's where it is suggested that a product marketed well enough will sell itself[15]. Whereas this might be the case for fast moving consumer goods, it is not the case for any other type of business and yet this "one size fits all" mantra is perpetuated with successive, standardised, new graduate "leaders of tomorrow". Diagnostic 17 is about how you sell to your customers and how connected your set of core values is to theirs. The diagnostic has four key sections with a series of questions that require an in depth response. Importantly, there is a need to view each measure in terms of its own stance within a market place, how active or rigorous it is in maintaining and growing that brand and the way that brand delights the customer and satisfies customer expectations.

---

[15] Robert Gunther 2008. "Peter Drucker - The grandfather of marketing: an interview with Dr. Philip Kotler", *Journal of the Academy of Marketing Science V37.1 pp17-19, March 2009.*

| DIAGNOSTIC 17 - SELLING TO YOUR CUSTOMER | |
|---|---|
| BRANDING | IS YOUR BRAND COMPLEMENTARY TO OR DISTRACTING FROM YOUR STRATEGIC INTENT |
| BRANDING | IS YOUR BRAND QUICK TO UNDERSTAND |
| BRANDING | IS YOUR BRAND PERSUASIVE |
| BRANDING | IS YOUR BRAND SATISFYING |
| AWARENESS | WHERE IS YOUR AWARENESS CONDUCTED |
| AWARENESS | WHAT HAVE YOU TANGIBLY GAINED BY DOING IT |
| AWARENESS | WHAT MEASURE OF SUCCESS HAS YOUR AWARENESS GIVEN YOU |
| SLOGANS | DO YOU HAVE "JINGLES" - WHY / WHY NOT |
| SLOGANS | DO YOU USE WORD BITES - WHY / WHY NOT |
| MOVING FORWARD | WHAT DOES YOUR SELLING SUCCESS LOOK LIKE |
| MOVING FORWARD | HOW ARE YOU GOING TO SELL INTO YOUR CHOSEN SPACE |

USE THIS PAGE AND MAP HOW YOU ARE PERFORMING AGAINST THESE MEASURES

*Diagnostic D1.17 - Selling to the Customer*

## Diagnostic 18

Diagnostic 18 looks at how your suppliers are performing against the same measures as Diagnostic 17. It is essentially an audit in terms of mapping inputs into the organisation against your own brand values and how the inputs of the organisation will actually influence your external brand values so, once again, same diagnostic but with a different perspective and once again to provide triangulation of the data generated.

| DIAGNOSTIC 18 - HOW YOU ARE BEING SOLD TO BY YOUR SUPPLIERS | |
|---|---|
| BRANDING | IS THEIR BRAND COMPLEMENTARY TO OR DISTRACTING FROM YOUR STRATEGIC INTENT |
| BRANDING | IS THEIR BRAND QUCIK TO UNDERSTAND |
| BRANDING | IS THEIR BRAND PERSUASIVE |
| BRANDING | IS THEIR BRAND SATISFYING |
| AWARENESS | WHERE IS THEIR AWARENESS CONDUCTED |
| AWARENESS | WHAT HAVE THEY TANGIBLY GAINED BY DOING IT |
| AWARENESS | WHAT MEASURE OF SUCCESS HAS THEIR AWARENESS GIVEN THEM |
| SLOGANS | DO THEY USE "JINGLES" - WHY / WHY NOT |
| SLOGANS | DO THEY USE WORD BITES - WHY / WHY NOT |
| MOVING FORWARD | WHAT DOES THEIR SELLING SUCCESS LOOK LIKE |
| MOVING FORWARD | HOW ARE THEY GOING TO SELL INTO THEIR CHOSEN SPACE - I.E. HOW ARE THEY GOING TO SELL TO YOU |

USE THIS PAGE AND MAP HOW YOU ARE BEING SOLD TO BY YOUR SUPPLIERS AGAINST THESE MEASURES

*Diagnostic D1.18 - How Your Suppliers are Selling to You*

## Diagnostic 19

Diagnostic 19 starts to look at the value add within an organisation and applies basic LEAN philosophy. Most organisations would today be expected to have formal quality management procedures and be running initiatives based around continuous improvement, LEAN or Six Sigma protocols. The key elements of LEAN include:

- The driving theme of "Getting more done with less"

- Identifying and eliminating non-value-adding activities throughout the process chain - to achieve a faster customer response time

- LEAN has been adopted extensively in larger organisations globally - but few smaller organisations have much familiarity with LEAN and few have implemented LEAN[16]

However, this isn't an exercise in whether you are ISO accredited or whether you have just won the latest quality accolade. From a leader's perspective in viewing your own organisation, how are you performing against reducing debt or defects, for example? What are you doing to remove unnecessary work movements throughout your organisation, both in terms of your materials and your people? These are significant strategic issues that must be addressed.

---

[16] This could be an indication of latent risk within a business b-ecosystem, where waste or crisis is hidden deep within the b-ecosystem being monitored.

| DIAGNOSTIC 19.1 - LEAN PHILOSOPHY | |
|---|---|
| REDUCING WASTE | HOW ARE YOU REDUCING WASTE IN YOUR ORGANISATION |
| REMOVING UNNECESSARY WORK MOVEMENTS | HOW ARE YOU REMOVING UNNECESSARY MOVEMENT OF PEOPLE |
| REMOVING UNNECESSARY WORK MOVEMENTS | HOW ARE YOU REMOVING UNNECESSARY MOVEMENTS OF MATERIALS (I.E. THE STUFF YOU DO AS A BUSINESS) |
| REDUCE WAITING TIMES | HOW ARE YOU REDUCING THE WAITING TIMES FOR THE WORK YOU DO AS A BUSINESS |
| REDUCE WAITING TIMES | HOW ARE YOU REDUCING THE WAITING TIMES OF YOUR MATERIALS (I.E. THE STUFF YOU DO AS A BUSINESS) |
| REDUCING WAITING TIMES | HOW ARE YOU REDUCING THE WAITING TIMES OF YOUR PEOPLE (I.E. HOW ARE YOU KEEPING YOUR PEOPLE PRODUCTIVELY ACITVE ALL OF THE TIME) |
| REDUCING EXCESS INVENTORY | HOW DO YOU KEEP INVENTORY (STOCK) TO A MINIMUM |
| REDUCE OVER PRODUCTION | HOW DO YOU PRODUCE JUST ENOUGH TO SATISFY YOUR CUSTOMER NEEDS |

USE THIS PAGE AND DEMONSTRATE HOW YOU PERFORM AGAINST THESE MEASURES

*Diagnostic D1.19.1 - LEAN Philosophy*

| DIAGNOSTIC 19.2 - LEAN TOOLS | |
|---|---|
| GETTING ORDER INTO YOUR WORKSPACE | HOW ARE YOU GETTING ORDER AND TIDINESS INTO YOUR WORK SPACE |
| | |
| REMOVING UNNECESSARY CLUTTER | HOW ARE YOU DISPOSING OF CLUTTER YOU DO NOT NEED |
| | |
| VISUAL CONTROLS | WHAT VISUAL CONTROLS AND COMMUNICATIONS DO YOU HAVE - HOW COULD YOU IMPROVE THEM |
| | |
| EFFICIENT WORK LAYOUT | HOW HAVE YOU MAXIMISED THE EFFICIENCY OF THE FLOW OF WORK IN YOUR WORKSPACE |
| | |
| STANDARDISED WORK | HOW DO YOU MAINTAIN STANDARDISATION OF WORK IN YOUR WORKSPACE |
| | |
| PREVENTATIVE MAINTENANCE | WHAT SCHEDULE OF MAINTENANCE DO YOU HAVE FOR YOUR CAPITAL ASSETS |
| | |
| PREVENTATIVE MAINTENANCE | WHAT SCHEDULE OF MAINTENANCE DO YOU HAVE FOR YOUR INTELLECTUAL ASSETS |
| | |
| PULL WORK FLOW | WHAT CUSTOMER PULL MECHANISMS TRIGGER THE FLOW OF WORK IN YOUR BUSINESS |
| | |
| RAPID RESPONSE | HOW DO YOU CHANGE RAPIDLY FROM ONE TASK TO ANOTHER IN YOUR BUSINESS |
| | |
| QUALITY DELIVERY (TO YOU) | HOW DO YOU ENSURE THAT THE FLOW OF GOODS, SERVICES AND INTELLECT INTO YOUR BUSINESS IS OF THE RIGHT QUALITY |
| | |
| CONTINUOUS IMPROVEMENT | HOW DO YOU IMPROVE ON YOUR FLOW AND SERVICE TO YOUR CUSTOMER - ALWAYS |
| | |

USE THIS PAGE AND DEMONSTRATE HOW YOU PERFORM AGAINST THESE MEASURES

*Diagnostic D1.19.2- LEAN Tools*

| DIAGNOSTIC 19.3 - THE LEAN PORTFOLIO | |
|---|---|
| MEASURING PERFORMANCE | HOW DO YOU MEASURE PERFORMANCE IN ALL AREAS OF THE BUSINESS AND IN ALL PARTS OF THE FLOW |
| MULTI TRAINED WORKFORCE | HOW DO YOU ENSURE YOUR WORKFORCE IS MULTI TRAINED AND COMPETENT TO UNDERTAKE ALL TASKS TO THE SAME LEVEL OF PERFORMANCE |
| FLEXIBLE & AUTOMATED (WHERE APPROPRIATE) | HOW IS YOUR BUSINESS FLEXIBLE (AGILE) AND WHAT APPROPRIATE AUTOMATION DO YOU HAVE IN PLACE |
| JUST IN TIME | HOW DOES YOUR ORGANISATION ENSURE THAT THE FLOW IN THE BUSINESS HAPPENS AT THE EXACT TIME IT NEEDS TO AT ALL POINTS IN THE BUSINESS ECOSYSTEM |
| SCHEDULING | HOW DO YOU SCHEDULE ALL ACTIVITIES AND FLOW IN YOUR BUSINESS ACCURATELY AND REALISTICALLY |
| REALISTIC WORK STANDARDS | HOW DO YOU ENSURE THAT THE STANDARDS OF WORK ARE REALISTIC WITHIN THE CONTEXT OF "YOUR SPACE" |
| WORKER EMPOWERMENT | HOW DO YOU EMPOWER YOUR WORKFORCE - HOW DO YOU ENSURE THAT THEY ARE EMPOWERED |
| ECOSYSTEM PARTNERS | WHAT TANGIBLE MEASURES DO YOU TAKE TO DEVELOP MEANINGFUL AND SYMBIOTIC PARTNERSHIPS WITH YOUR PARTNERS |

USE THIS PAGE AND DEMONSTRATE HOW YOU PERFORM AGAINST THESE MEASURES

*Diagnostic D1.19.3 - The LEAN Portfolio*

## Diagnostic 20

Diagnostic 20 is about providing a strategy sanity check. For example, what is it that you are trying do to and why are you trying to do it? Diagnostic 20 should be straightforward to answer but often organisations lose strategic intent in day-to-day operational necessities and it is always wise to keep referencing back to your core intent.

| DIAGNOSTIC 20 - THE BUSINESS ECOSYSTEM SANITY CHECK | |
|---|---|
| WHAT ARE YOU TRYING TO DO | |
| WHY ARE YOU TRYING TO DO IT | |
| HOW ARE YOU TRYING TO DO IT | |
| HOW DO YOU KNOW ITS WORKING | |
| HOW COULD YOU IMPROVE IT | |
| HOW DO YOU KNOW YOU HAVE IMPROVED IT | |
| USE THIS PAGE AND COMPLETE THE BUSINESS ECOSYSTEM SANITY CHECK | |

*Diagnostic D1.20 - The Business Ecosystem Sanity Check*

## Diagnostic 21

Diagnostic 21 provides insight into the use of and benefits from the technology employed within an organisation. To reduce risk, companies have consistently put the same standard information technology solutions in place. This forces everyone to design and operate the same process and this,in turn, drives organisations to the same middle ground. By the end of the twentieth century, information technology accounted for some half of all global business capital expenditure[17] and yet it remains the highest risk point in the b-ecosystem after sales, the least likely to be fully integrated into the b-ecosystem and associated with the highest levels of failure, incompatibility and worker frustration.

It is a very simple process to determine whether, for example, your technology minimises human error and reduces time and cost. In theory an organisation should be able to answer 'yes' to all of these elements. Often, however, this is not necessarily the case and significant waste is incurred in organisations becoming slaves to IT and not stewards of quality and customer service.

[17] Nicholas G. Carr, IT Doesn't Matter, *Harvard Business Review*, May 2003.

| DIAGNOSTIC 21 - THE TECHNOLOGY AUDIT | | |
|---|---|---|
| MINIMISES HUMAN ERROR | YES | NO |
| WHY / WHY NOT | | |
| REDUCES TIME | YES | NO |
| WHY / WHY NOT | | |
| REDUCES COST | YES | NO |
| WHY / WHY NOT | | |
| INCREASES EFFICIENCY | YES | NO |
| WHY / WHY NOT | | |
| PROVIDES STANDARDISATION | YES | NO |
| WHY / WHY NOT | | |
| ENABLES COMMUNICATION | YES | NO |
| WHY / WHY NOT | | |
| PROVIDES AN INNOVATION / CREATIVE LEVER | YES | NO |
| WHY / WHY NOT | | |
| DRIVES ROBUST RECORD KEEPING & ARCHIVING | YES | NO |
| WHY / WHY NOT | | |
| PROVIDES ACCURATE & APPROPRIATE TRACEABILITY | YES | NO |
| WHY / WHY NOT | | |

USE THIS PAGE AND COMPLETE THE TECHNOLOGY AUDIT ON YOUR BUSINESS

*Diagnostic D1.21 - The Technology Audit*

# Diagnostic 22

Diagnostic 22 looks at the whole business operation and aims to determine how suppliers are performing against simple key matrices in terms of on time delivery, order fulfillment, cash-to-cash cycle times and total operational supply costs. This diagnostic asks you to check your suppliers' current performance, find areas for improvement and find or identify what is going to sustain that improvement into the future.

| DIAGNOSTIC 22 - THE BUSINESS ECOSYSTEM PERFORMANCE METRICS | | | |
|---|---|---|---|
| | CURRENT PERFORMANCE | IMPROVED PERFORMANCE | SUSTAINING ACTION |
| ON TIME DELIVERY (TO COMMITTED DATE) | WHY | HOW | WHAT ARE YOU GOING TO DO ABOUT IT |
| ORDER FULFILLMENT LEAD TIME | WHY | HOW | WHAT ARE YOU GOING TO DO ABOUT IT |
| CASH TO CASH CYCLE TIME | WHY | HOW | WHAT ARE YOU GOING TO DO ABOUT IT |
| TOTAL ECOSYSTEM MANAGEMENT COST | WHY | HOW | WHAT ARE YOU GOING TO DO ABOUT IT |

USE THIS PAGE AND NOTE HOW YOUR BUSINESS ECOSYSTEM PERFORMS AGAINST THESE METRICS AND WHAT YOU NEED TO DO TO IMPROVE AND SUSTAIN THE PERFORMANCE

*Diagnostic D1.22 - The Business Ecosystem Performance Metrics*

## Diagnostic 23

Diagnostic 23 focuses on ranking your business performance against nine key performance points and also, once ranked, how or what has to be done to sustain and improve performance. The diagnostic looks into areas such as data management, inventory management, capital assets etc. and forms the hard core of any internal value audit.

| | DIAGNOSTIC 23 - RANKING BUSINESS ECOSYSTEM PERFORMANCE | | |
|---|---|---|---|
| | | CURRENT PERFORMANCE (1-10) | SUSTAINING / IMPROVING ACTION |
| 1 | ESTABLISH & MANAGE RULES | | |
| 2 | ASSESS PERFORMANCE | | |
| 3 | MANAGE DATA | | |
| 4 | MANAGE INVENTORY (STOCK) | | |
| 5 | MANAGE CAPITAL ASSETS | | |
| 6 | MANAGE TRANSPORTATION | | |
| 7 | MANAGE BUSINESS ECOSYSTEM CONFIGURATION (DESIGN) | | |
| 8 | MANAGE REGULATORY COMPLIANCE | | |
| 9 | PROCESS (FLOW) SPECIFIC ELEMENTS | | |

USE THIS PAGE AND RANK HOW THE PARTICIPANTS IN YOUR BUSINESS ECOSYSTEM ARE PERFORMING AGAINST THESE MEASURES AND HOW / WHAT YOU NEED TO DO TO MAINTAIN OR IMPROVE PERFORMANCE

*Diagnostic D1.23 - Developing Business Ecosystem Performance*

## Diagnostic 24

Diagnostic 24 focuses on developing a sustainable or resilient future for the organisation. Business resilience begins with having the right leadership, innovation and sustainability principles that are customer centric (see Figure 1.2.12).

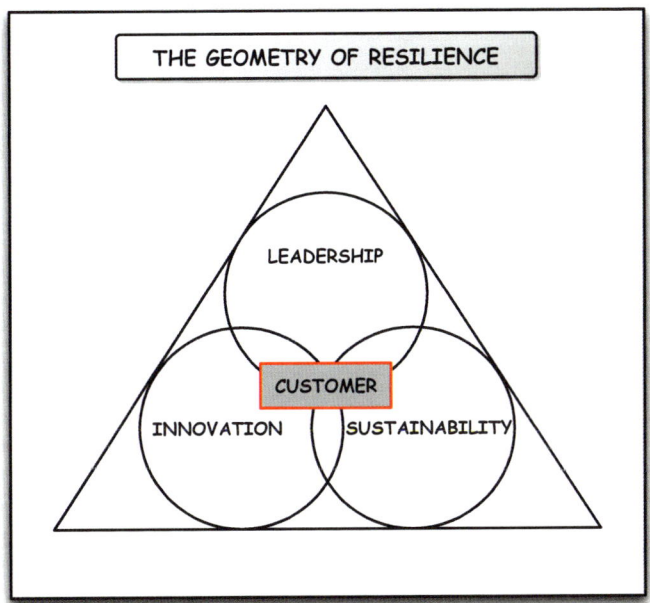

*Figure 1.2.12 - The Geometry of Business Resilience*

In the context of the "long term viability" concern of sustainability, the crux of the issue is around an organisations ability to move into the intended future strategic position (this is the focus of the third book in the series). Issues such as, is the business "right-on time-every time", the auditing of customer requirements and understanding why customers buy from your organisation are critical. In this diagnostic the "yes" and "no" element is important. "Maybe" does not suffice as an answer because it injects a level of ambiguity. The "how" or the "why" should provide clear insight into these key elements moving forward.

| DIAGNOSTIC 24 - MOVING TO A SUSTAINABLE & RESILIENT BUSINESS ECOSYSTEM | | | |
|---|---|---|---|
| | | | HOW / WHY |
| 1 | IS YOUR ECOSYSTEM RIGHT - ON TIME - EVERY TIME | YES | NO | |
| 2 | DO YOU AUDIT & UNDERSTAND YOUR ACTUAL CUSTOMER REQUIREMENTS | YES | NO | |
| 3 | DO YOU AUDIT & UNDERSTAND WHY YOUR CUSTOMERS BUY FROM YOU | YES | NO | |
| 4 | DO YOU AUDIT & UNDERSTAND THE CURRENT LEGITIMATE CAPACITY OF YOUR ECOSYSTEM FLOW - WHAT IS IT | YES | NO | |
| 5 | DO YOU AUDIT & UNDERSTAND THE CONSTRAINTS ON YOUR ECOSYSTEM | YES | NO | |
| 6 | DO YOU AUDIT & UNDERSTAND THE POINTS AT WHICH YOUR ECOSYSTEM IS VUNERABLE | YES | NO | |

USE THIS PAGE AND RANK HOW YOUR ECOSYSTEM PERFORMS AGAINST THESE QUESTIONS

*Diagnostic D1.24 - Moving to a Sustainable & Resilient Business Ecosystem*

The 24 diagnostics provide an opportunity to think differently and deeply about your organisation. The instructions around the diagnostics are deliberately not overly prescriptive to encourage thought and reflection and, hopefully, discussion with colleagues. Any of the diagnostics that you may have decided didn't apply to your organisation, or were too difficult, or you didn't really understand, are the most important for you to consider. All 24 of the diagnostics apply to all organisations be they large or small, commercial or not for profit, manufacturing or services, private or government. The process of completing the diagnostics will probably have increased your awareness of certain aspects of your organisation and challenged assumptions so it is suggested that you return to the diagnostics and continue to add insights as they occur.

The diagnostics should also have generated consideration of the degree of alignment between the strategies of your business, your suppliers and your customers. Moving forward with a b-ecosystem awareness, alignment and collaboration may present opportunities and differentiation strategies where it is possible to take advantage of the concept that the whole is bigger than the sum of its parts.

Following are two concluding diagnostics that ask you to self-assess your responses to the diagnostics and your awareness of the way your business relates to the b-ecosystem in which it operates. These summary diagnostics provide a useful snapshot of the areas in which you are most and least confident and also provide the opportunity to generate ideas for how to maintain your performance where you are confident and how to improve performance where you are not as confident.

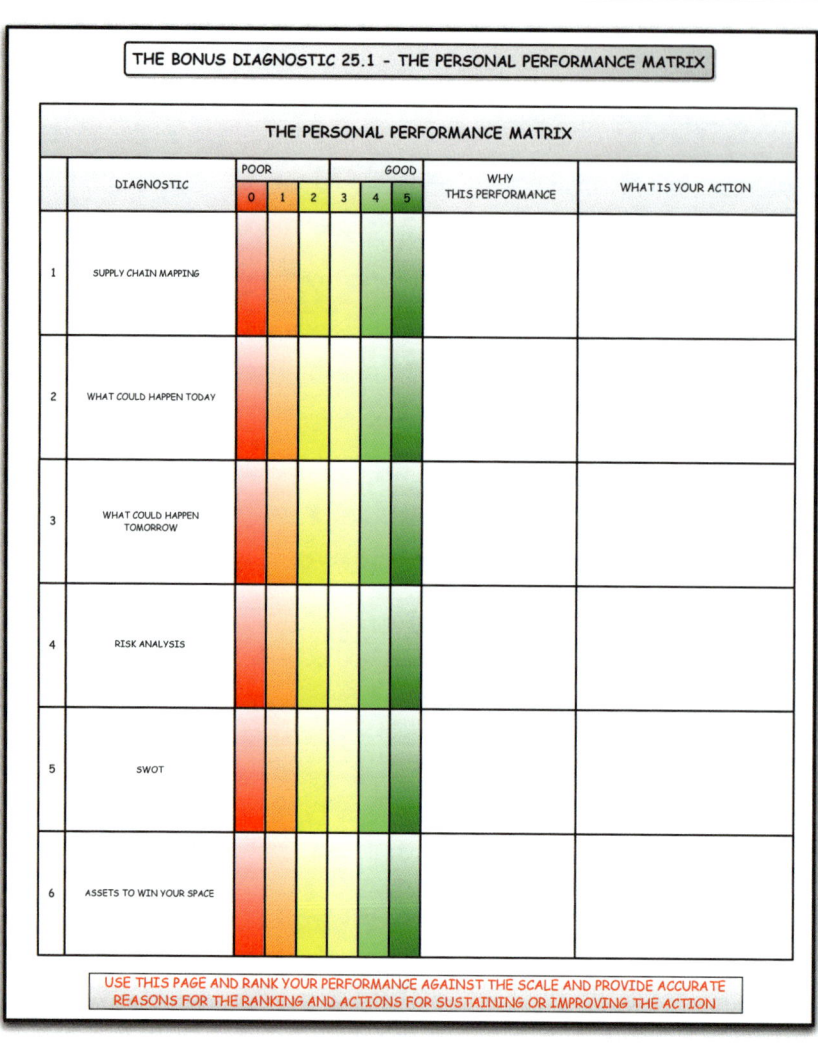

THE BONUS DIAGNOSTIC 25.1 - THE PERSONAL PERFORMANCE MATRIX

THE PERSONAL PERFORMANCE MATRIX

| | DIAGNOSTIC | POOR | | | | GOOD | | WHY THIS PERFORMANCE | WHAT IS YOUR ACTION |
|---|---|---|---|---|---|---|---|---|---|
| | | 0 | 1 | 2 | 3 | 4 | 5 | | |
| 1 | SUPPLY CHAIN MAPPING | | | | | | | | |
| 2 | WHAT COULD HAPPEN TODAY | | | | | | | | |
| 3 | WHAT COULD HAPPEN TOMORROW | | | | | | | | |
| 4 | RISK ANALYSIS | | | | | | | | |
| 5 | SWOT | | | | | | | | |
| 6 | ASSETS TO WIN YOUR SPACE | | | | | | | | |

USE THIS PAGE AND RANK YOUR PERFORMANCE AGAINST THE SCALE AND PROVIDE ACCURATE REASONS FOR THE RANKING AND ACTIONS FOR SUSTAINING OR IMPROVING THE ACTION

*Diagnostic D1.25.1 - The Personal Performance Matrix*

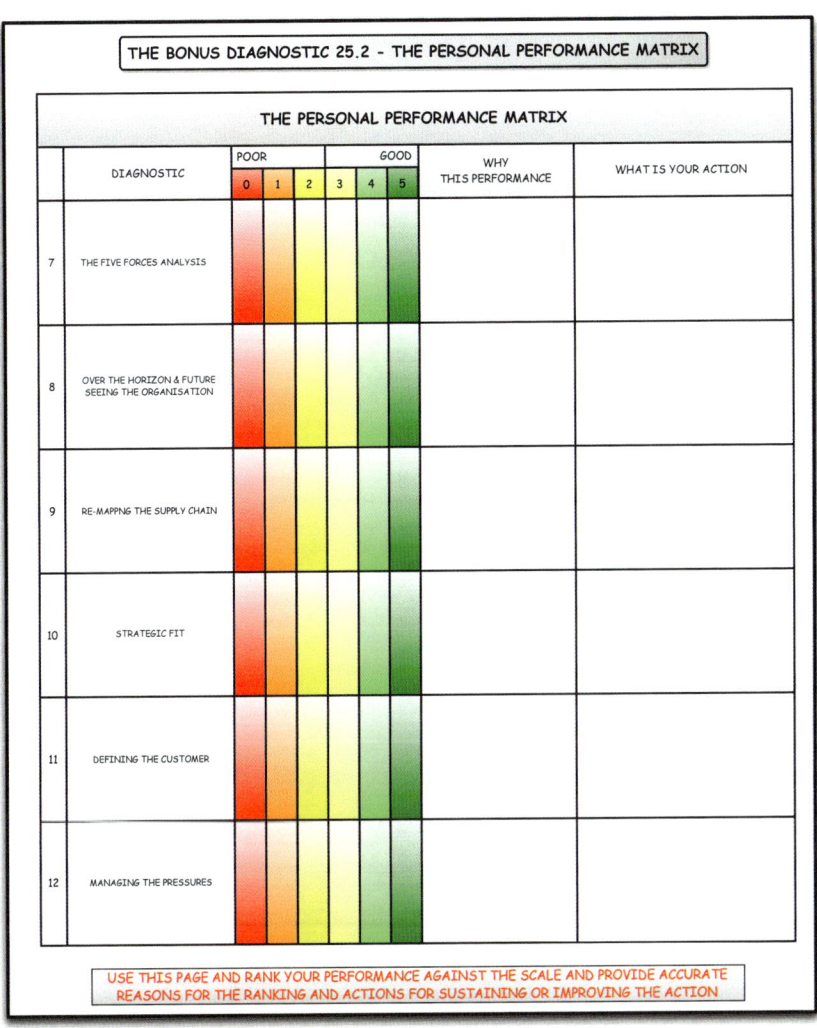

## THE PERSONAL PERFORMANCE MATRIX

| | DIAGNOSTIC | POOR | | | | GOOD | | WHY THIS PERFORMANCE | WHAT IS YOUR ACTION |
|---|---|---|---|---|---|---|---|---|---|
| | | 0 | 1 | 2 | 3 | 4 | 5 | | |
| 7 | THE FIVE FORCES ANALYSIS | | | | | | | | |
| 8 | OVER THE HORIZON & FUTURE SEEING THE ORGANISATION | | | | | | | | |
| 9 | RE-MAPPNG THE SUPPLY CHAIN | | | | | | | | |
| 10 | STRATEGIC FIT | | | | | | | | |
| 11 | DEFINING THE CUSTOMER | | | | | | | | |
| 12 | MANAGING THE PRESSURES | | | | | | | | |

THE BONUS DIAGNOSTIC 25.2 - THE PERSONAL PERFORMANCE MATRIX

USE THIS PAGE AND RANK YOUR PERFORMANCE AGAINST THE SCALE AND PROVIDE ACCURATE REASONS FOR THE RANKING AND ACTIONS FOR SUSTAINING OR IMPROVING THE ACTION

*Diagnostic D1.25.2 - The Personal Performance Matrix*

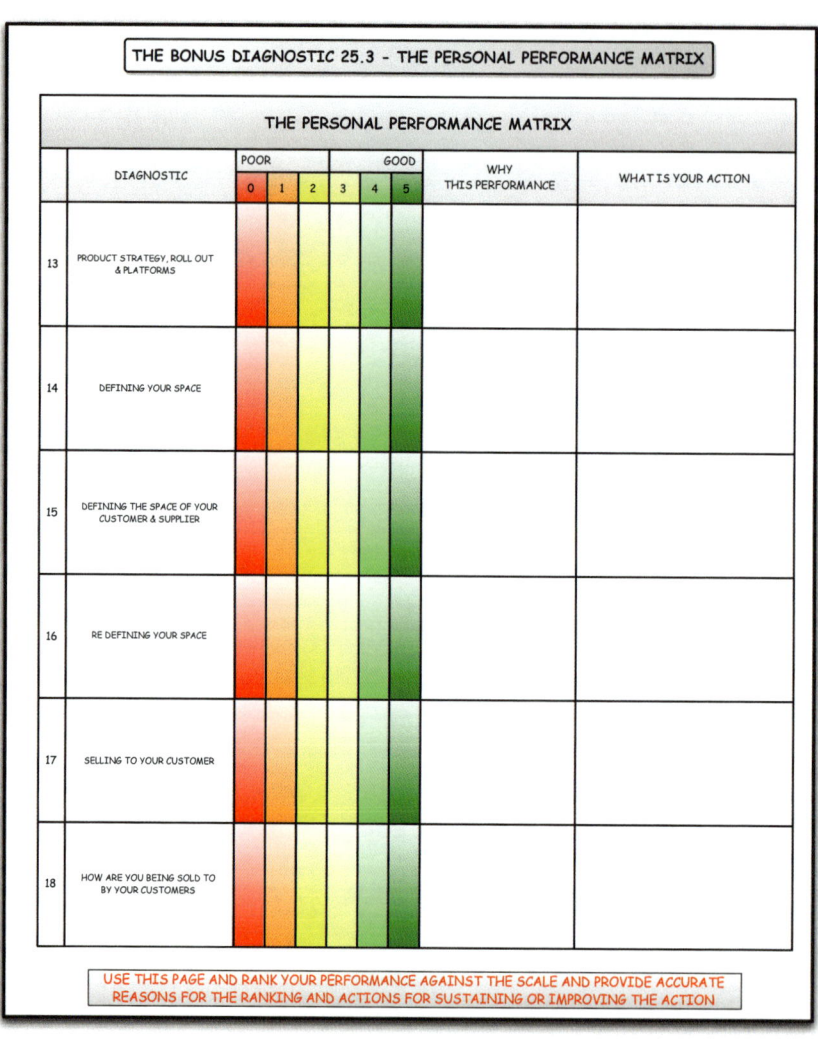

THE BONUS DIAGNOSTIC 25.3 - THE PERSONAL PERFORMANCE MATRIX

THE PERSONAL PERFORMANCE MATRIX

| | DIAGNOSTIC | POOR | | | | GOOD | | WHY THIS PERFORMANCE | WHAT IS YOUR ACTION |
|---|---|---|---|---|---|---|---|---|---|
| | | 0 | 1 | 2 | 3 | 4 | 5 | | |
| 13 | PRODUCT STRATEGY, ROLL OUT & PLATFORMS | | | | | | | | |
| 14 | DEFINING YOUR SPACE | | | | | | | | |
| 15 | DEFINING THE SPACE OF YOUR CUSTOMER & SUPPLIER | | | | | | | | |
| 16 | RE DEFINING YOUR SPACE | | | | | | | | |
| 17 | SELLING TO YOUR CUSTOMER | | | | | | | | |
| 18 | HOW ARE YOU BEING SOLD TO BY YOUR CUSTOMERS | | | | | | | | |

USE THIS PAGE AND RANK YOUR PERFORMANCE AGAINST THE SCALE AND PROVIDE ACCURATE REASONS FOR THE RANKING AND ACTIONS FOR SUSTAINING OR IMPROVING THE ACTION

*Diagnostic D1.25.3 - The Personal Performance Matrix*

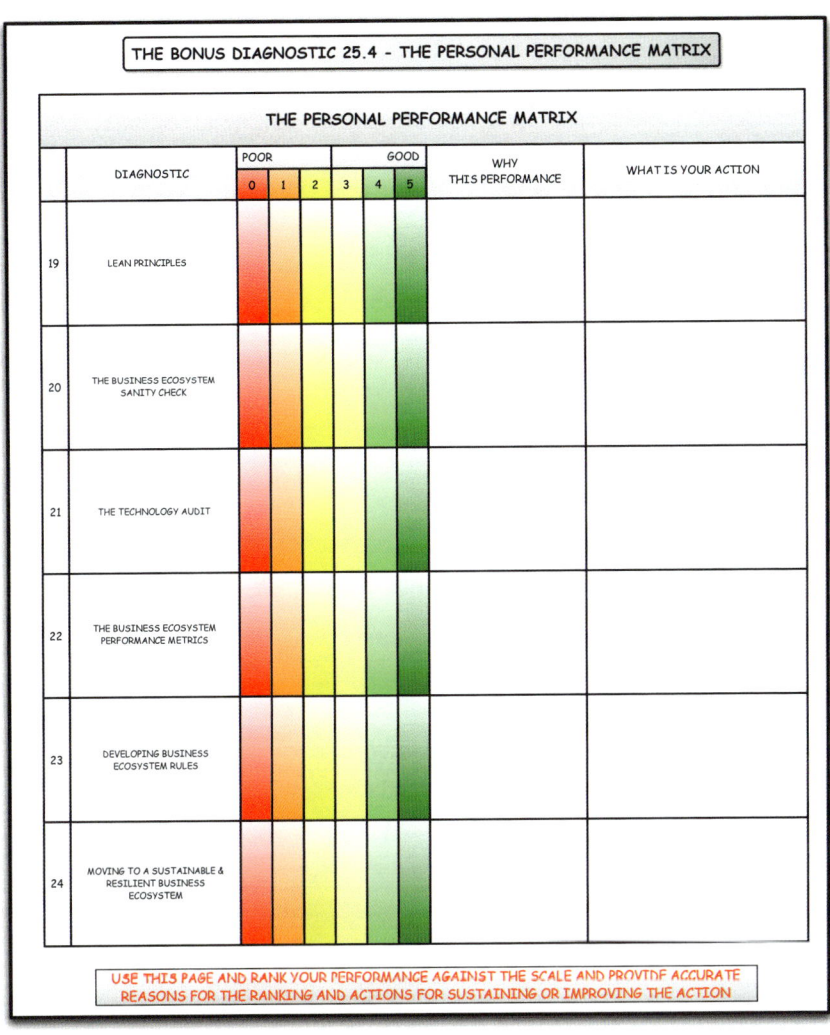

| | DIAGNOSTIC | POOR | | | | GOOD | | WHY THIS PERFORMANCE | WHAT IS YOUR ACTION |
|---|---|---|---|---|---|---|---|---|---|
| | | 0 | 1 | 2 | 3 | 4 | 5 | | |
| 19 | LEAN PRINCIPLES | | | | | | | | |
| 20 | THE BUSINESS ECOSYSTEM SANITY CHECK | | | | | | | | |
| 21 | THE TECHNOLOGY AUDIT | | | | | | | | |
| 22 | THE BUSINESS ECOSYSTEM PERFORMANCE METRICS | | | | | | | | |
| 23 | DEVELOPING BUSINESS ECOSYSTEM RULES | | | | | | | | |
| 24 | MOVING TO A SUSTAINABLE & RESILIENT BUSINESS ECOSYSTEM | | | | | | | | |

THE BONUS DIAGNOSTIC 25.4 - THE PERSONAL PERFORMANCE MATRIX

THE PERSONAL PERFORMANCE MATRIX

USE THIS PAGE AND RANK YOUR PERFORMANCE AGAINST THE SCALE AND PROVIDE ACCURATE REASONS FOR THE RANKING AND ACTIONS FOR SUSTAINING OR IMPROVING THE ACTION

*Diagnostic D1.25.4 - The Personal Performance Matrix*

## THE B-ECOSYSTEM MATRIX

| | DIAGNOSTIC | POOR | | | | GOOD | | WHY THIS PERFORMANCE | WHAT IS YOUR ACTION |
|---|---|---|---|---|---|---|---|---|---|
| | | 0 | 1 | 2 | 3 | 4 | 5 | | |
| 1 | DO YOU HAVE A CLEAR (SIMPLE) VIEW OF YOUR STRATEGIC POSITION AND MARKET TRENDS | | | | | | | | |
| 2 | HOW GOOD IS YOUR SUPPLY NETWORK, ITS COMPETENCY & CAPABILITY MOVING FORWARD | | | | | | | | |
| 3 | WHAT RISK IS THERE IN YOUR BUSINESS ECOSYSTEM | | | | | | | | |
| 4 | HOW GOOD IS YOUR TECHNOLOGICAL ADVANTAGE | | | | | | | | |
| 5 | HOW GOOD IS YOUR INNOVATIVE CAPABILITY AND THAT OF YOUR BUSINESS ECOSYSTEM | | | | | | | | |
| 6 | HOW COMFORTABLE / CONFIDENT ARE YOU ABOUT THE FUTURE SUSTAINABILITY & RESILIENCE OF YOUR ORGANISATIONS | | | | | | | | |

USE THIS PAGE AND RANK YOUR PERFORMANCE AGAINST THE SCALE AND PROVIDE ACCURATE REASONS FOR THE RANKING AND ACTIONS FOR SUSTAINING OR IMPROVING THE ACTION

*Diagnostic D1.26 - The B-ecosystem Matrix*

## Summary of the Diagnostic Program

Through objectively conducting the 24 diagnostics and the two summary diagnostics, an organisation should gain insight into how it is performing now, where there are gaps and, indeed, what they should be doing about those gaps.

The diagnostics provide an opportunity to develop a perspective on your business as if "standing on the outside". Shadow walling is likely to provide a significant judgmental bias during the process and, whether the diagnostics are conducted as a leadership program, a collective team effort, an "individual group" effort, where individual business leaders do it autonomously and the answers are brought together for discussion, is at the discretion of the user. However, Act 1 Scene 3, goes on to discuss previous results from these diagnostics and discuss some of the key considerations in larger detail. Suffice to say, how good or how bad your results are initially, you are not alone and knowing where you are now is the first step in moving to where you want to be.

# ACT 1 - SCENE 3

# EVALUATING THE CURRENT BUSINESS DYNAMIC -

# AN INSIGHT INTO WHAT THE DIAGNOSTICS HAVE REVEALED

## Introduction

The diagnostics presented in Scene 2, have been applied in numerous and diverse organisations, both large and small, and have often been reported as being the catalyst for change within those organisations. As mentioned in Scene 1, the diagnostics have been run in a number of countries and particularly in Australia where, through government programs and, over many years in the Executive Master of Business Administration program at the Sydney Business School, successive leaders of business have applied these diagnostics within their own sectors with some quite remarkable results. The initial picture derived from the diagnostics, however, was a cause for concern for many of these organisations. This Scene 3, presents some generalised feedback from a number of the previous diagnostic workshop sessions. This feedback provides a model for how the results of the diagnostics can be reviewed as a whole, to establish whether existing strategies and practices across your business, your suppliers and your customers are aligned. The feedback is also provided as a benchmark, in terms of where other businesses found themselves before the diagnostics provided a catalyst for change. The feedback is accompanied by further explanation of the dynamics driving the change process towards a more holistic b-ecosystem approach to business.

## Background to the Studies and Collection of the Results

The data for this work has been derived from the many and varied focus groups and individual participants who have completed the diagnostics since 2010. Due to the longevity of the diagnostics, the sample set can be determined to be random, or as near as possible to a random representation, of business.   All of the participants have been senior officers within their organisations and, as such, were those involved in the strategic aspects of their businesses.

**The Rationale and Design of the Diagnostics**

The diagnostics have been developed over more than 30 years of my professional and academic career, from proven business modeling, analysis and due diligence methodologies. The diagnostics had previously been used successfully in many private businesses improvement consultation programs and supplier selection protocols globally.   The positive results from running the diagnostics, along with the positive response to the diagnostics in these consultation and improvement processes, prompted the formalisation of the diagnostics into a set, which is provided in Scene 2 for self-administration and, on which this feedback is based.

The diagnostics were developed around five key b-ecosystem themes, these being:

1. Analysing Strategic Positioning and Market Trends

2. Analysing Supply Networks, Supply Competency and Capability

3. Analysing the Potential Risk Inherent within Supply Networks

4. Analysing Technology

5. An Insight into Innovation

By developing key themes for the diagnostics it was possible to map the overall capabilities of the participants. There is no suggestion that there were not some world class participants, however, it is the sample mean in this case that provides the core indicator of performance not selected "best (or indeed worst) in class".

**Key Feedback From the Diagnostic Workshops - An Indication of Competitive Readiness**

MindMapping techniques, applied to the key data, allow associations to be made that assist in developing a big picture view. Figures 1.3.4 and 1.3.5 illustrate MindMaps of the key findings of some groups of participants who have completed the diagnostics to date.

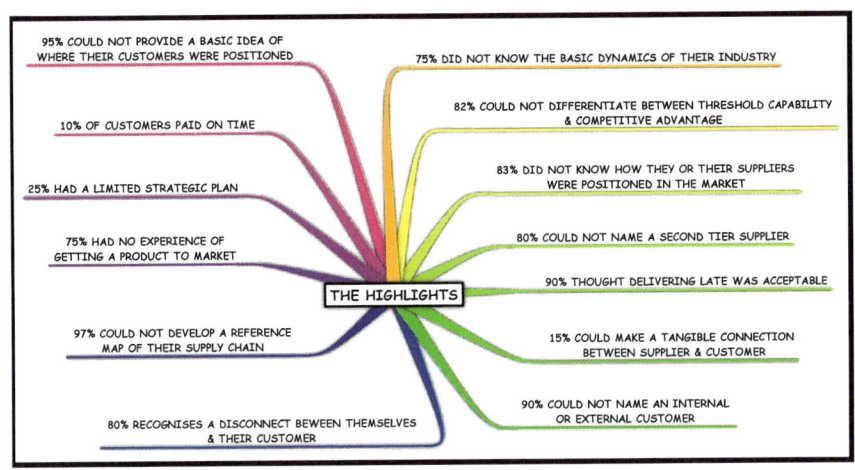

*Figure 1.3.4 A MindMap of the Key Findings of the Participants to Date*

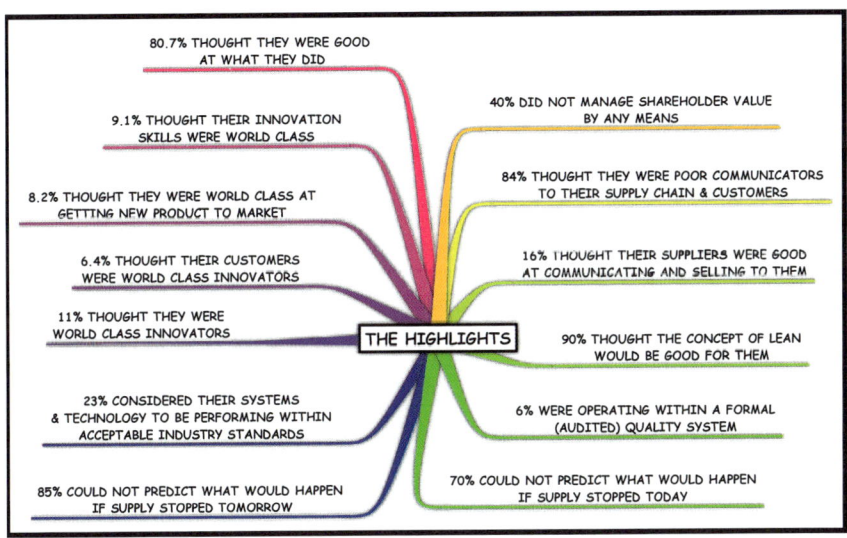

*Figure 1.3.5 A MindMap of the Key Findings of the Participants to Date*

## An Analysis of the Feedback From the Diagnostic Participants to Date

Overall, the feedback from participants to date suggests that there is a significant disconnect between supplier and customer. This represents a significant disturbance in the b-ecosystem. As previously discussed, a disconnect between supplier and customer exposes all businesses to risk. This risk can be as elementary as gaps in understanding of customer requirements leading to failures to meet customer need or, indeed, more complicated gaps such as a lack of predictability around the potential impact of changes, in any one supplier or customer, on the other interconnected businesses. Lack of customer focus is evident in the near universal response that, delivering "right-on time-every time" to the customer was only a consideration, not an imperative. There was also an undercurrent of many participants indicating that, as employees of the company, they are being instructed by their leaders that service level expectations were higher than the organisation could or would bear. This indicates a disturbing trend of organisational disconnection and devaluation towards customer focus. Typically, this is accompanied by a cost-cutting mantra that further erodes the focus on the customer, the focus on differentiation and, eventually, the ability to compete. By working to build better connections between suppliers and customers, niche opportunities and other differentiated value-added business expansion opportunities may emerge. It cannot be stated too many times that:

*In a free market only one business can be the cheapest, the rest have to differentiate.*

*A customer focus is imperative for effective differentiation.*

The results also suggest that business dynamics are typically not monitored and/or understood. Most businesses have monitoring processes, however, often they are monitoring the wrong things for their business. Monitoring processes are, all too often, another casualty of the "one-size-fits-all" modern management approach, that is currently proliferated by much business education, that also leads to the siloing of business functions, the focus on separate short-term targets and the focus on costs not customers. Too often, the focus of business management is on optimising independent processes, rather than optimising the overall achievement of the business purpose of profitably delivering to customer requirements in such a way as to keep existing customers and win new customers.

The feedback also indicated that there is often a significant lack of formal business and quality management systems, underlying a lack of investment in these systems coupled with underinvestment in technology and people. Quality management seems to have been relegated to operational habit rather than being utilised as a strategic tool. Continuous improvement as a competitive necessity is not understood and processes are often not in place to find and reduce unnecessary waste within the business while increasing value to the customer.

Whereas most organisations would publicly indicate that they are performing within industry recognised performance measures, core performance matrices are not cascaded through the larger b-ecosystem and key performance indicators are not consistent.

It is evident that few organisations have any consistent experience of getting new products to market and most are ready and willing to offer "re-gifted" product without customer consultation. This one action alone could be the initial and destructive factor to drive customers away from current business partners.

There is little evidence of any mid to long term planning. Corporate and supply strategy could not be articulated by most of the focus group participants to date, suggesting it is lacking in most cases. Significantly, the feedback suggests most organisations are unable to map their supply network further than a few core (close to home) suppliers and there is no risk assessment concerning possible factors that could stop the flow of supply. Although collaboration and integration concepts are recognised, there is little evidence to suggest that these principles are actually being practiced. This raises the risk that a supply network could become inoperable because of the inability of foundation suppliers to deliver seemingly unimportant products and services. This is disturbing because there appears to be little, if any, comprehension by businesses that they are operating within a b-ecosystem and that by changing one element, (albeit small), then the entire system changes.

Furthermore, most foundation suppliers appear to have been "hanging in there" for a considerable period of time and recent changes in supplier engagement and communication protocols by focal companies could be the death knell for many such organisations. These repercussions have the potential to be felt throughout the b-ecosystem. Participants in the use of the diagnostics to date, have provided significant qualitative data concerning the current operational readiness of the foundation supply base and enabled a profile of risk to be developed.

## Traditional Supply Relationship Management and Current Supply Risk

In considering the risk in the foundation base of many business supply networks, a duality of key factors have been identified that have a direct impact on current networks. These key factors are:

1. Whether a critical mass of the supply base exists and whether key knowledge capital is limited and contracting in specialist areas

2. Whether a paradox exists where many surviving suppliers do not posses the threshold capabilities necessary to engage with current customer procurement matrices into the future

Although these factors have been identified, perversely, within the context of traditional models of supplier development and procurement, business as a whole is doing nothing wrong. It has been common wisdom to accept that supply networks are complicated so efficiencies and value can be added to a supply network if the focal company targets its attention on the first couple of tiers of supply and then shifts the role of responsibility for managing lower tiers to its own suppliers. This rationale has been extended to include the use of good technology, for example Enterprise Resource Planning (ERP), to communicate throughout the supply base. Figure 1.3.1 illustrates the basic concept of bow tie thinking and the ERP cascade.

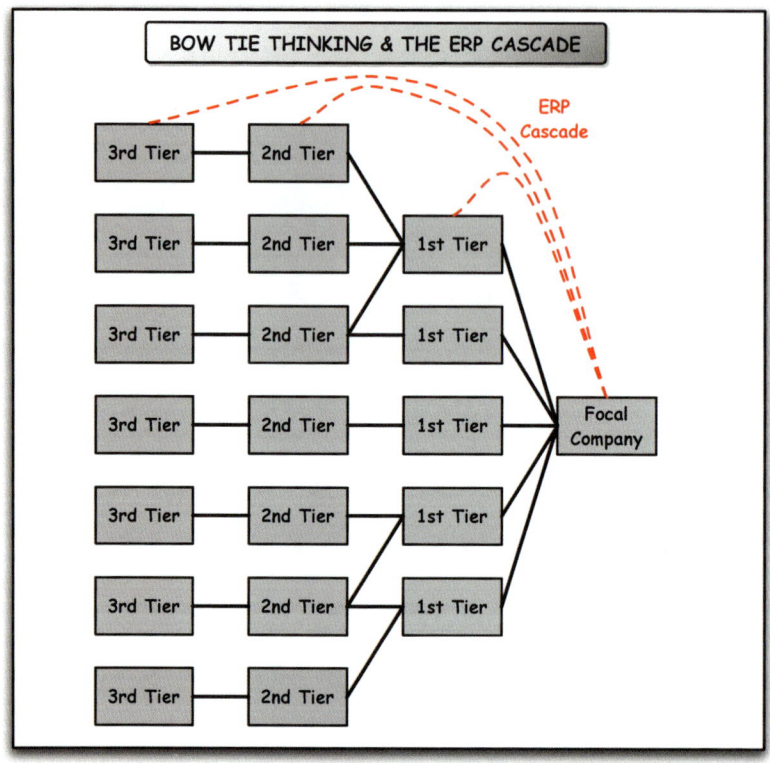

*Figure 1.3.1 The Basic Concept of Bow Tie Thinking and the ERP Cascade*

Shifting the role of responsibility has been extensively exploited as a principle for focusing supply management attention on "where it needs to be focused" (i.e. core, key top level suppliers). By taking a slightly different view of supply mapping and effectively turning the map through $90^{\circ}$, it is possible to visualise a case where top tier suppliers (i.e. tiers 1 and 2) effectively block any view of other suppliers due to their magnitude compared with suppliers at lower levels. It is reasonable to assume that no amount of "Over-the-Horizon" (OTH) strategy is going to impact on the current understanding of the supply network because the focal company cannot achieve enough levitation to see over the blockers. Figure 1.3.2 illustrates the basic concept of role shifting blocking the view of supply in the context of Over-the-Horizon thinking.

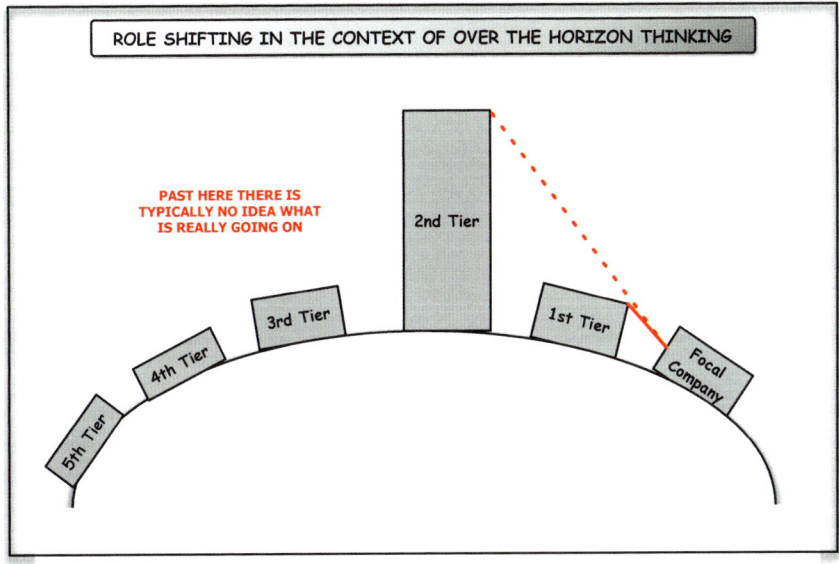

*Figure 1.3.2 An Illustration of Role Shifting in the Context of Over The Horizon Thinking*

Importantly, there appears to be a significant disconnect between the space that a focal company and its Tier 1 and Tier 2 suppliers occupy within a supply network and the corresponding operational, communication and quality framework that suppliers in tiers further from the focal company operate within. Basically, there is an assumption that the same rules apply throughout the supply network but, in reality, different tiers may be following different rules. This may be summarised within a scenario where a focal company and its local area supply network (i.e. the top tier suppliers) operate within one local active supply network and, at the same point of time, lower level suppliers operate within their own active local area supply network. As a result, a two-way disconnect, therefore, appears to exist where the focal company assumes (usually incorrectly) that someone else is taking care of other (often perceived to be less important local area supply networks), while, at the same time, local area supply networks outside of the core cluster (i.e. lower tiers of suppliers) typically assume (usually incorrectly) that the focal company is their customer. A myth of supply integration is developed and an operational mantra of "management through intentionally disregarding the overall network", is adopted because it's a convenient axiom that is never challenged. Put simply, there is no evidence to suggest that full supply integration has ever been established within any full supply network. Figure 1.3.3 illustrates the myth of supply integration.

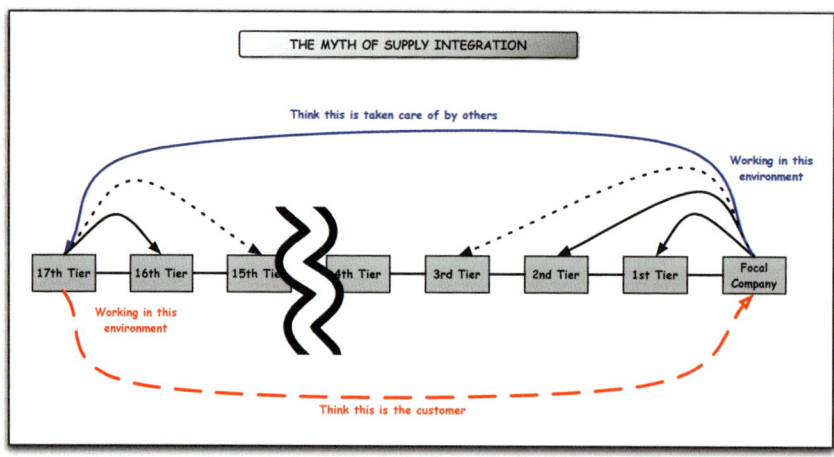

*Figure 1.3.3 The Myth of Supply Integration*

Research has indicated that OEM's have typically focused attention on Tier 1 and Tier 2 suppliers and lost visibility of lower level suppliers by outsourcing the management and responsibility of the lower level suppliers to their Tier 1 and Tier 2 suppliers. The outsourcing of management and responsibility has created a significant disconnect and compounded risk in business networks. Remarkably, this scenario is accepted as "best practice" under recognised supply management protocols.

Business capability and supplier engagement trends have changed considerably in recent times. Once robust supply networks have been eroded and capacity reduced. OEM[18] engagement patterns have changed so that they now may often preclude existing suppliers in favour of new, alternative partners. A consistent pattern of tighter future supplier engagement requirements has become apparent amongst diagnostic participants. The pattern emerging consists of four key points:

1. Need to Move to Larger Lower Risk Suppliers - larger organisations are being preferred as suppliers because they are perceived to present less risk within the supply network

2. Need for Transparency - transparency and traceability within the supply network are considered to be significant issues for companies seeking sustainable supply

---

[18] In the context of this work, an OEM is defined as the central hub or node of a business ecosystem - however, depending on perspective, this node can be viewed differently by different network partners at different points in time and space

3. Need for Systems - because of the need for transparency, traceability and also consistency, there is a requirement for formal business and quality management systems to be embedded within the supply network

4. Need for Continuation of Supply - a key driver is continuity of supply, typically summarised as "right - on time - every time"

While these requirements would appear to be a positive response to addressing risk in the supply network, with little awareness of the need to understand the entire b-ecosystem before making changes the impact of such, even seemingly positive measures to reduce risk may have unexpected consequences and could actually contribute to triggering the supply risk that the measures are being implemented to avoid.

The potential for unintended consequences occurs because the focus, when considering supply, is usually on the main interaction node within a network, with the result that there is no attention given to the seemingly unimportant "lower level" foundation organisations that have a critical role within the network. There is an assumption, encouraged by the models often used to represent supply networks such as the bow tie model, that foundation suppliers are numerous and have little effect in the overall competitive and operational readiness of a supply network. However, if the data from the work to date is extrapolated, then it becomes apparent that many business supply networks could be significantly below the performance capability necessary to be considered robust or sustainable. Importantly, the combined mass of small suppliers within a supply network could be "the perfect risk accelerator" and represent a clear and present danger in terms of performance realisation. Indeed, previous participants in the diagnostics have demonstrated that they could identify a significant risk hidden within the foundation supply base of their b-ecosystem. This risk has become critical to be aware of and manage because there is a risk posed to supply through three key interrelated issues. These three key issues are:

1. The changes in supplier engagement requirements to meet risk reduction policies

2. The emerging paradox in the quality of supplier availability

3. The gaps in key supply capability

**The Changes in Supplier Engagement Requirements**

As previously described, there is an increased requirement for many OEM's (traditional focal companies) to lower the overall risk in their supply network. The typical risk reduction frameworks have included demands of greater transparency within the networks, the need for more formal (and often externally audited) business systems and quality management frameworks, and the need for guaranteed continuity of supply driving a preference for larger suppliers. Compliance with these requirements, however, may increase the costs of smaller suppliers and negatively impact on the viability of these businesses. Loss of smaller grass roots or foundation suppliers providing critical parts may pose significant risk to supply with an impact throughout the b-ecosystem.

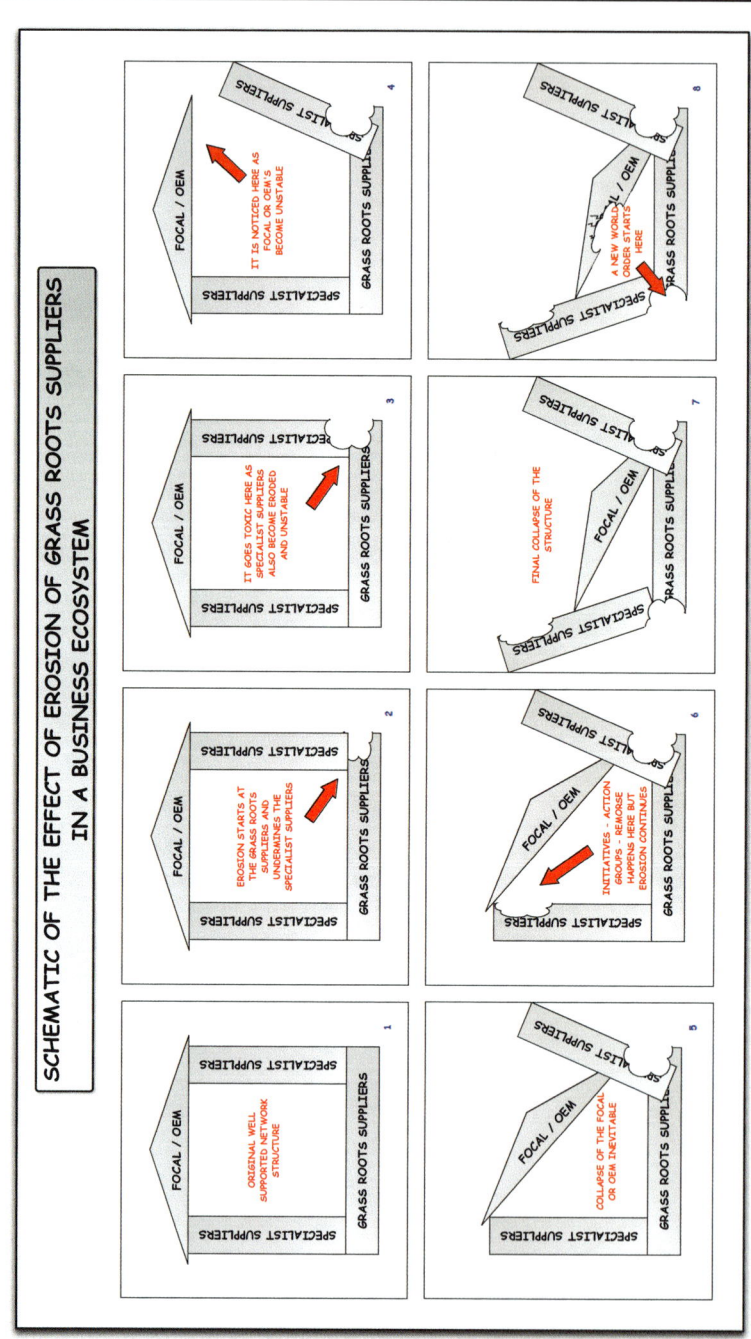

*Figure 1.3.4 - The Effect of Erosion of Grass Roots Suppliers*

## The Emerging Paradox in Supplier Availability

Whereas the change in supplier engagement requirements may, at first sight, appear to be a move in the right direction, a paradox is rapidly emerging of a best set of worst suppliers. This is because it is not uncommon to find that those organisations that have survived, thus far, are those that have not invested in technology, business systems and people. Put simply, the financial structure is comparatively lower for organisations that don't invest in their business and, during crisis, this allows them to hang on longer than more heavily invested businesses that needed higher levels of revenue to break even. As such, a significant proportion of the foundation supply base may now be considered to be the least qualified to deliver into the new and reemerging supply networks. Similarly, successive exercises in cost cutting and restructuring have often left a band-aided shell of a once viable supplier. This, however, may not be visible to other businesses, particularly those further removed, in the supply network.

## Gaps in Key Supply Capability

Many companies contracted significantly during the recent crisis. Consumer demand dried up and supply channels often became little more than a trickle of work. Due to this contraction, as demand has increased typical procurement matrices such as contract value as a ratio of supplier turnover, cannot be met by new or incumbent suppliers (i.e. the prospective supplier is now too small to qualify to supply into a network, because its turnover is now lower and the contract value is proportionally larger).

As companies contracted, they let go of many key "knowledge rich" employees. Many became consultants but, due to market forces, entered a hyper-competitive marketplace and, as such, many became under-employed and others have moved on altogether. A lack of availability and/or under-employed availability, generates considerable risk in the foundation supply of the b-ecosystem because many businesses are left with a choice of one or none. Importantly, many of the knowledge rich people are no longer in positions within the supply network, yet many customers are placing orders on organisations with the belief that the organisation concerned has the knowledge capital itself when, it fact, it may be outsourcing to third party providers.

**The Tsunami Over the Horizon**

From the work to date, it is becoming evident that:

1.  In the future, continuity of supply often cannot be guaranteed due to uncertainty of supply in lower and foundation tiers. This is exacerbated by changes in procurement policy and regulations that further erode any already shaky foundation supply bases and, as such, the total b-ecosystem.

2.  Since a major point of risk for many businesses is within the foundation base, larger "focal" companies run the real risk of developing the best set of worst suppliers; suppliers that do not have the capability of delivering right - on time - every time.

## Conclusions

In many cases, the organisations that have been able to weather "the storm" successfully over recent years and the successive changes in the market, are less able to supply now and, in many cases, may be poorly positioned to do so into the future. The time has come for those that are still operational to overhaul their organisations and thoroughly examine their interrelationships with other business and make their b-ecosystem road worthy for the journey ahead.

The findings to date indicate that there is a significant risk present within current b-ecosystems and that this risk is still typically hidden due to businesses concentrating on their major immediate partners and trusting that these major partners will do the same at other levels in the supply network. Remarkably, this situation has been made manifest because supply and procurement professionals have adopted recognised and accepted "old world" protocols and focused on partners closest to them (i.e. Tier 1 and Tier 2) and expected these partners to do the same throughout the b-ecosystem. This assumption is as dangerous as it is negligent and demonstrates a serious error in leadership standards.

Similarly, the feedback indicates that businesses have a disconnect with their customers. The resulting loss of the ability to differentiate can lead a business to compete in the mediocre commoditised middle ground and miss opportunities to retain and win customers through adding value and delivering continuous improvement.

Put simply, business have followed standard principles of management and leadership and a new focus and direction is needed if many businesses are to reduce risks to supply and find sustainable markets that they are best suited to contest. Following the practices of competitors, or the mystical words of advisors who are one step removed from the operation, becomes dangerous because this will drive business into the grey middle ground of the hyper-competitive market. To save face, however, particularly in the eyes of "outside" observers, lacklustre leaders will continue to argue that they have done nothing wrong. By "doing nothing wrong", however, they now run the risk of continuing to develop the best set of worst partners and worst set of "best practices".

*Perhaps it is now worth going back to your Personal Performance Matrix and reconsidering the rankings that you have provided giving consideration to complex business dynamics and how the concept of partnership may need to be redefined.*

**Coming Next**

Act 1 provided the first set of diagnostics. These enable participants to establish a picture of the position and health of their business and its associated network. In the next series, Act 2 provides a datum that consists of tools, methodologies and mentoring to develop a differentiation capability to meet the huge pressures on businesses to find innovative solutions to remain competitive in ways that are both ethical and sustainable.

# PREQUEL

## How Did We Get Here?

The business environment has significantly altered since the Global Financial Crisis (GFC) of 2008. There is an awareness of increased complexity, uncertainty and, for many businesses, vulnerability with multiple challenges to retaining competitiveness and ongoing viability. The GFC was different to recessions that had been experienced, and mostly survived, before. The speed and severity of the GFC was as unexpected as it was unprecedented. Trust had gone out of "the financial system" and business stopped. Most companies were in free fall. There was no market, no money, no supply, no flow. The only references available - classical analysis based on old world reference points - didn't work. The impact on our businesses, our customer's businesses, our suppliers businesses and our competitor's businesses was not understood. Our analysis and our decisions at the time reflected the disorientation of being in unknown territory without a map; there was simply no reference point or datum for what was going on, nor, for the pattern of regrowth for those that survived. A new approach was needed.

The GFC demonstrated the high degree of interconnectedness that now characterises organisations and markets and how exposed businesses are to disturbances; with events triggered by defaults on mortgages in the USA having a devastating impact on completely different industries in completely different countries around the world. As supply is now characterised by complexity, the term "supply chain" may be somewhat deceptive. The word 'chain' suggests a linear, consecutive connection moving sequentially from one step to the next. Supply no longer works this way. Few businesses, however, are fully aware of the many integrated and interdependent relationships in which they are linked.

At the time of the GFC, the businesses still standing found themselves operating in an environment where the competitive landscape and supply flow were substantially altered; as was their business and the businesses of their suppliers and customers. Recovery, also, was not to provide a return to "what was".

The knock-on effect of the reduction of personal and business lines of credit in the GFC, was a massive contraction in markets for both manufactured goods and services. This rendered the supply chain systems of the manufacturing and service industries on a "razors edge" unable to operate in a marketplace of such unprecedented turbulence. Over time, both large and small businesses failed as they found themselves unable to react or plan to match negative customer demand.

Almost perversely, as some sectors were coming out of their initial crisis others had yet to face their first, due to the lag or 'long tail' effect through the larger system. Almost like a dam stopping the flow of a river, the first area to be drowned was that area closest to the blockage of the dam wall, or closest to the customer who no longer had the money with which to purchase. Over time, however, the blockage backs up and those further away from the cause of the blockage eventually also become consumed in the same flood waters (see Figure PL.1).

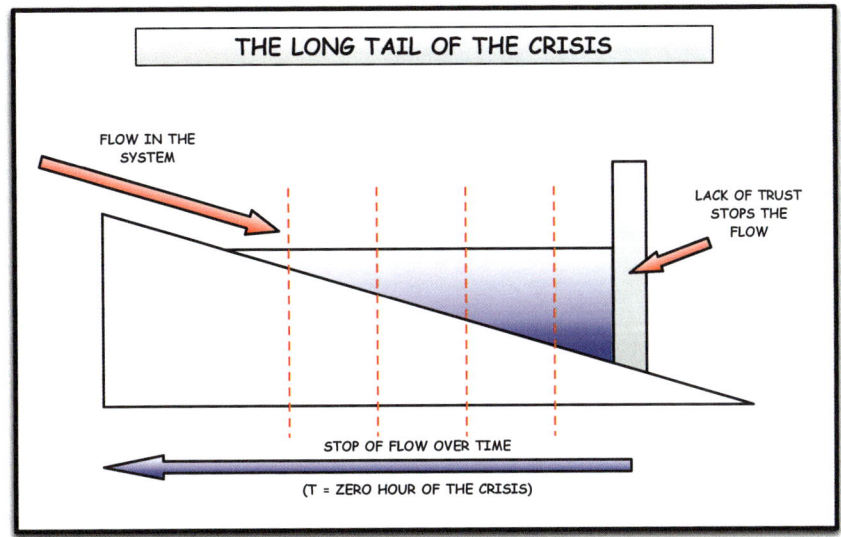

*Figure PL.1 - A Schematic of the Long Tail Effect of the Crisis*

For those organisations that were able to contract sufficiently, the next great challenge for their leaders was focusing on the reconfiguration of their operations as business returned. There was no precedent for the level of uncertainty and level of risk involved in this regrowth process, or indeed from the depths from which the regrowth now needed to emerge. The contraction had, for many, resulted in downsizing and with it loss of staff, loss of customers, loss of suppliers, loss of markets and loss of credit.

At the time, and privately, many business leaders were acknowledging that demand had dropped by as much as 80% operating from normal throughput and that this extreme event confounded them, their suppliers and, indeed, their customers.

At the height of the crisis it was imperative that businesses retained as much of their markets as they could while, ideally, broadening their customer base in order to remain viable. In effect, businesses of all sizes were adopting small company agility principles and tactics of accepting any work that was available at the time. The practical problem was that everyone was trying to do the same thing in a shrinking market where there was only a finite amount of business and extreme and savage competition. An additional problem was the significant contraction in the pool of suppliers and resources. For some sectors resource starvation became critical and contracts were being lost because of supplier inability to supply on-time, to specification and within expected risk profiles.

My work, at the time of the crisis, focused on reassembling businesses and supply networks to keep them going while making sense of what was happening. The concept of Dip Dynamics was introduced, based on observations of the time, to describe the impact of the crisis and the risks in the subsequent regrowth phase of business[19]. The set of business diagnostics discussed in Act 1 Scene 2, was used to assist businesses in the rebuilding of their networks. This rebuilding model was used in a program for the Australian Government and also moved out across Asia and into Europe and the USA. Subsequent commissions developed market intelligence gathering diagnostic tools along with further diagnostic tools intended on moving the business forward.

---

[19] The crisis was happening "live" and all around us, there was no time for rigorous "philosophising" or theory postulations - we needed to now what was happening and what was likely to happen next, with no contextual reference for where we were at any point. For example, we would tell ourselves one day that things could not get any worse and the next day we were invariably proven wrong.

## The Principle of Dip Dynamics

Dip Dynamics suggests that, due to a lack of resource availability after significant downsizing, organisations will not recover to where they were prior to the crisis because the dynamics of their business and total business system have changed.  The popular belief at the time of the GFC, that there would be a wealth of resources available on the upturn, was not realised.  For those organisations that had either been able to downsize their operations sufficiently and rapidly or had simply ceased trading, a "perfect storm" of new challenges emerged.  If they had ceased trading, usually there was nothing subsequently.


There are four stages in the dip and recovery dynamic.  Many business sectors appeared to experience a process of Dip Dynamics and depending on the tier of supply, some companies are still at one of the four stages of dip and recovery.  These stages are:

1.  The Drop Zone

2.  The Slap Zone

3.  The Balance Zone

4.  The Reconfiguration Zone

## The Drop Zone

The Drop Zone can be considered to be the first part of Dip Dynamics. It's where the drop in the flow occurs and it is where the economic viability of the business becomes challenged by external forces. From running at 100% normal capacity, (this is operating at the maximum they could achieve based on their capability in a strong economic environment; not to be confused with optimum efficiency) their marketplace rapidly retracts, causing the need to cut business radically. The dynamic is such that, initially, if a company has to cut its business then they are forced to cut their resources, inventory, people and supply chain by more than the size of the cut in business. This is because there is significantly more value in their supply chain in terms of out-standing orders to suppliers, work in progress and stock, etc. Demand from end customers drops off as they stop buying, however, typically suppliers have overbought and have excess inventory, based on projections of the pre-crisis market, so their orders to suppliers stop suddenly because this excess inventory is in place when the end customers stopped buying. There is lag in the supply cycle between supplies being ordered and these supplies being delivered (lag time or long tail). Orders may already have been in place from customers to suppliers and these take time to be processed and delivered while the market is already grinding to a halt. These orders need to clear though the system and this takes time to accomplish. As such, business is paralyzed; there is no activity for some time because the bullwhip effect caused during this time is settling down and there is no need for them to place orders lower down the chain for a depressed market that just isn't buying.

## The Slap Zone

The Slap Zone is the period when the real effect of what has happened in the Drop Zone is felt. This is where no orders are being placed and most businesses are considering or actually laying off staff because they are unable to pay all of their bills with the level of business activity. Since staff are usually the highest single rapidly reducible cost for the business they are often the first casualty when the business contracts and shrinks (i.e. stopping equipment does not save money in real terms but stopping people instantly saves money).

Within the Slap Zone, customers that are still in business and still manufacturing goods or providing services, will be working with the inventory that they had "over-ordered" in the "normal market" and sitting on re-stocking orders, as there is no need to increase inventory or maintain it at the previous levels when little is going "out of the door".

This period may be different for different types of businesses and different sectors. For example, as companies rethink their future strategies and tactics they may place on hold plans to build a new office or factory and this has an early impact on companies manufacturing building products and the building industry as a whole. The effect is felt later in time by the usual supplier of materials for the company that has reconsidered its expansion because, although they have stopped the expansion, they haven't stopped business altogether.

The characteristics of the Slap Zone will also vary depending upon the type of crisis. For a long and slow recession where the market slows gradually over a period of time, the Slap Zone will be different to one where the market has stopped suddenly due to a lack of credit.

**The Balance Zone**

Once the businesses that have survived and continued to trade have passed through the Slap Zone, there will be a need for them to reorder stock (i.e. re-fill the system or re-commence the flow) because they will have used up their remaining inventory. Some commentators may see this as the earliest green shoots of recovery. Unfortunately, this does not appear to be the case. While there is the need to bring some new orders back through the supply network, work typically bounces along for a while because it is not possible to establish the true, new market size and traditional forward planning protocol gives way to reactionary ordering. The Balance Zone is a re-calibration of the market; an adjustment that's required for the new level of trading that has emerged from the Slap Zone.

During the recommencement of the flow in the Balance Zone it is important to note that the trading isn't level or linear but is, instead, non-linear and fluctuating. Typically, ordering patterns will be more disjointed than before the crisis started. For example, instead of ordering five tonnes of a raw material a customer may only order two tonnes as they do not want to be left in the same position of holding excess inventory that they were in at the time the dip started (i.e. customers don't want to have massive amounts of inventory with nowhere for it to go). This is even more prevalent in markets for goods with limited shelf life. Many business leaders believe that their businesses are going to grow again and get straight back up to where they started prior to the drop but, there is now a different dynamic. Businesses that were at the top of their capability have now decimated their workforce, stock and working capital not to mention their line of credit. In effect, business has been forcefully reconfigured.

Figure PL.2, depicts the principle of Dip Dynamics as it applies to the capacity of and demand on a business when plotted against time. The premise is that, over time, a business will go through the Drop Zone (i.e. the effect of a crisis), then there follows periods of operation within the Slap Zone, the Balance Zone and the Reconfiguration Zone. Passage through all of the zones indicates that the business has stayed agile and responsive enough to market conditions and so has remained viable. Business economics may also mean that a company drops out at any time due to the load placed upon it, either being bought up by continued aggressive competitor reaction or closing its doors due to an inability to withstand further market shrinkage (i.e. they became insolvent).

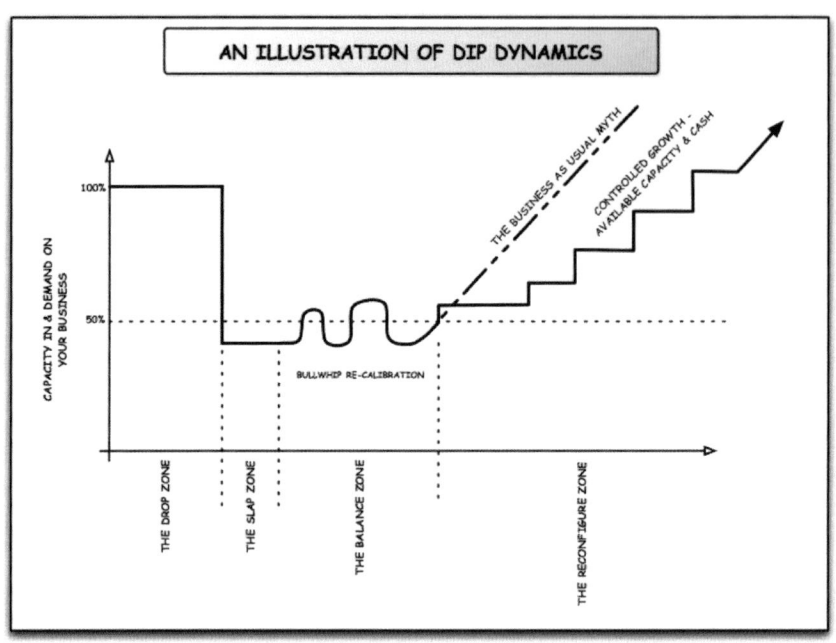

Figure PL.2 - The Principles of Dip Dynamics

## The "Business As Usual" Myth of Business Growth

There is a hypothesis generally that growth post a crisis will be linear. It is typically argued that customers will suddenly start ordering again at the same rate as they did prior to the crisis. However, this is not necessarily the case due to the scale and severity of the particular crisis.

For a customer to be able to place an order they must have a path of credit available and they must have somewhere for the order to come from and somewhere for the product or service to be delivered to (i.e. they need supply and a customer).

"Business as usual" describes the path of processing being the same on the way out of the crisis as it was on the way in (i.e. manufacturing or processing capacity is the same, orders for the goods or services are the same and the people required to fulfill that order are still in place). However, since the company has already passed through the Slap Zone, where they have been forced to contract the business in order to remain viable, major tangible and intangible assets such as people capacity and capability or materials are now gone from the system. The likelihood is that the skills required to operate at the same performance level will take considerable time to re-establish into the system. This presupposes that the line of credit that the company had before the crisis is available. If the company has been trading close to the point of bankruptcy and cash-flow is problematic, then the credit line may not be readily available. In this case the order is not likely to be honoured unless payment is made "up front" thus affecting or disrupting business flow throughout the system.

In short, businesses cannot simply pick up just where it left off, even if it was able to "weather the storm" of a major crisis.

**The Reconfiguration Zone**

If the hypothesis of "business as usual" is questionable at best, then there must be something else that will replace it, in order to achieve some level of growth over some period of time. This is the Reconfiguration Zone, where the aggregate gradient of the path of growth is limited by the available capacity (people and equipment) and credit available.

The growth that is achieved here is marked with caution rather than optimism, consolidating existing customers, market shares and volumes before growing to new customers and markets (i.e. an extremely risk averse decision environment). Therefore, rather than recovery being the mythical and magical linear growth, in actuality it is a stepped growth pattern where there is consolidation then growth, then more consolidation then growth and so on.

An important aspect of this stepped growth is that it will always be at a slower growth rate than the theoretical linear one.

**Differing and Distorted Viewpoints**

Depending upon how far away a commentator is from the customer and the market, they will have differing views and different beliefs on the market status. The lag, or long tail, may not be recognised by people who are not in that business but, rather, in different parts of the network. As the viewpoint of the commentator gets further away from the customer, so the level of distortion increases. Economists may see what an order book is like, be it full or sparse, and may believe that they are seeing the effects of the situation today. In reality, they may be seeing a knock on effect of a situation that developed three months ago due to supply chain lag. The full order book may lead a more removed commentator to assume that the rest of the supply network is robust and functioning, however, that order may be satisified through excess stock or work in progress already contained within the OEM, so there is no flow through the network. Too often, while commentators removed from a business are talking about signs of market recovery, the organisation itself is asking, "What market?".

This reverse bullwhip effect has the effect of instilling a false sense of well-being into stakeholders and a belief set of "she'll be right". This contributes to further problems such as a lack of confidence when expected flow doesn't eventuate, potential disruptions to business if a supplier unexpectedly fails and governments placing the wrong measures and incentives in the wrong places in the supply network. There is the possibility that there could be companies running out of critical resources during the upturn due to a lack of suppliers capable of delivering competitively. All of these potential outcomes lead to further decline in the network. This may, in turn, open up opportunity for those organisations that have a competitive drive to win markets, adding increased competitive pressures to already struggling businesses.

**Distortion in the Network Through Uneven Impacts of a Crisis**

An additional dynamic in the Dip Dynamic process is that of some industries being in growth while other tiers in their supply are in crisis. In Australia, for example, during the crisis the oil and gas industries and even mineral exports experienced growth. This created a compound effect where an OEM is in growth while lower tier suppliers are struggling, creating a bigger gap in supply and a significantly larger risk in the network because of this dynamic (see Figure PL.3).

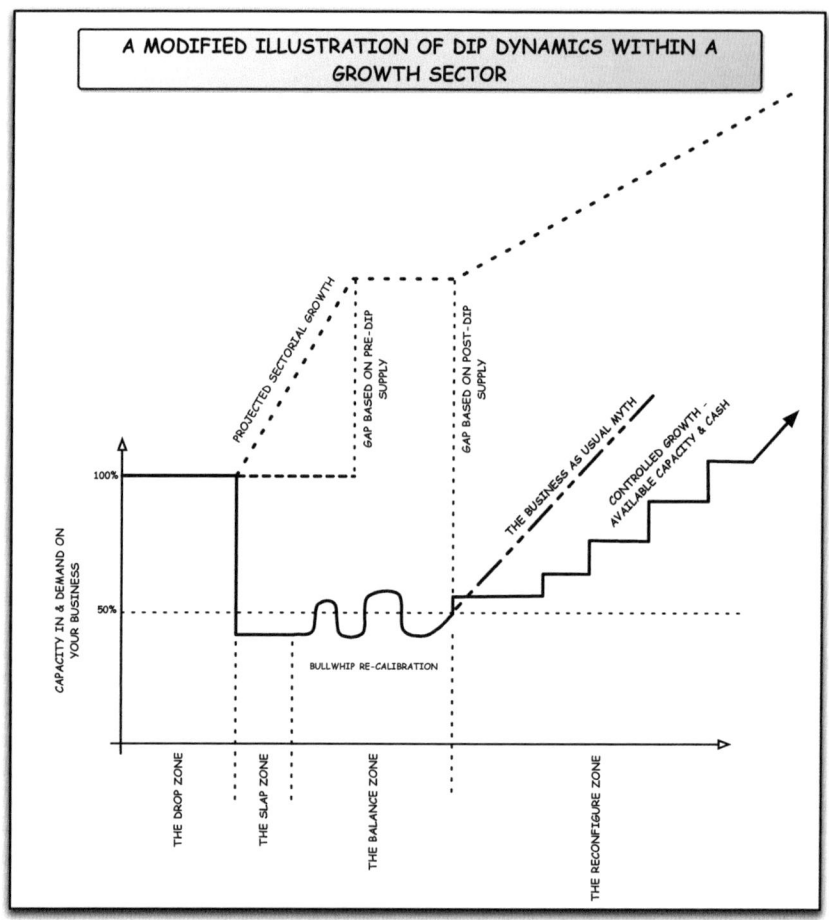

*Figure PL.3 - Dip Dynamics and the Affect of Growth in Certain Sectors*

A myth of supply chain theory is the existence of end-to-end configuration within the supply network. What is also needed for efficiency is end-to-end communication within the supply network. Supply networks, however, are inherently secretive and are inherently deceitful. The reality is that, if a business is suffering then the last people that they want to tell is other businesses within their network because customers won't buy from a suffering business for fear of warranty or of failing by association, suppliers won't supply for fear of not getting paid, banks will withhold and/or recall payment and debt for fear of being left with debt, the workforce will become disgruntled and start to look for more secure employment and any or all of these additional difficulties will contribute to the likelihood of the demise of the organisation. The maintenance of deceit is, therefore, a necessary by-product of the way supply has been structured.

Complexity within the supply network provides the opportunity for an alternative structure that would allow that, while one company is struggling, the rest of the network could fill the gap and continue. Given time within that network, to function at the level at which it is capable of functioning, the struggling organisation may be able to come back as a viable player. The notion of a linear chain with successive suppliers, all playing "pass-the-parcel" in a consecutive chain is not conducive to longevity, cooperation or indeed sustainability. Recognition that your business chain is, indeed, linear is recognition that the chain is only as strong as the weakest link. Any weakening of those links by any stop in flow means that the flow to your business is at risk of stopping as well. Complexity can provide an opportunity to structure more robust supply networks and such "non-rational" supply networks will be discussed in the sequel to this work.

**The Impact of OEM Disruption on the Network of Supply**

Distortion also exists with regard to the impact of the loss of an OEM on the supply network and community in general. When a supply network is severely disrupted, typically, the community at large become aware of job losses in the OEM through an announcement by the OEM itself. Other cuts made through the first, second and third tiers of supply, however, generally are not announced as loudly. This distorts understanding of the true impact of the loss or downsizing of an OEM on the larger supply network. Real data relating to the so called "indirect loss of jobs" is, typically, almost impossible to obtain.

While involved in economic regeneration projects working with inward investment agencies and foreign direct investment agencies in many countries, it became apparent that neither they, nor the politicians, were advertising the fact that they were all too aware of the impact of an OEM closing and that, the ratio of job losses through supply tiers remained reasonably consistent across industry sectors and countries. Data collated over this time showed that for every job lost in the OEM, five jobs would be lost in Tier 1 suppliers. That 5:1 ratio would stay the same in the second tier. So, for every job lost in Tier 1, a further five jobs would be lost in Tier 2. For every jobs lost in Tier 2, three jobs would be lost in Tier 3. For every job lost in Tier 3, once again three jobs would be lost in Tier 4. In Tier 5 however, seven jobs would be lost for every job lost in Tier 4. The explanations provided for this large loss at Tier 5, suggested that the support industries not directly related to the OEM, so not usually considered in terms of the impact of an OEM closing, such as hairdressers, sandwich bars, taxi drivers and the local pub, would not be able to operate because there was no longer a supply of money from anyone else in the system more directly connected with the OEM. Figure PL.4 shows the above job loss ratios through the supply system.

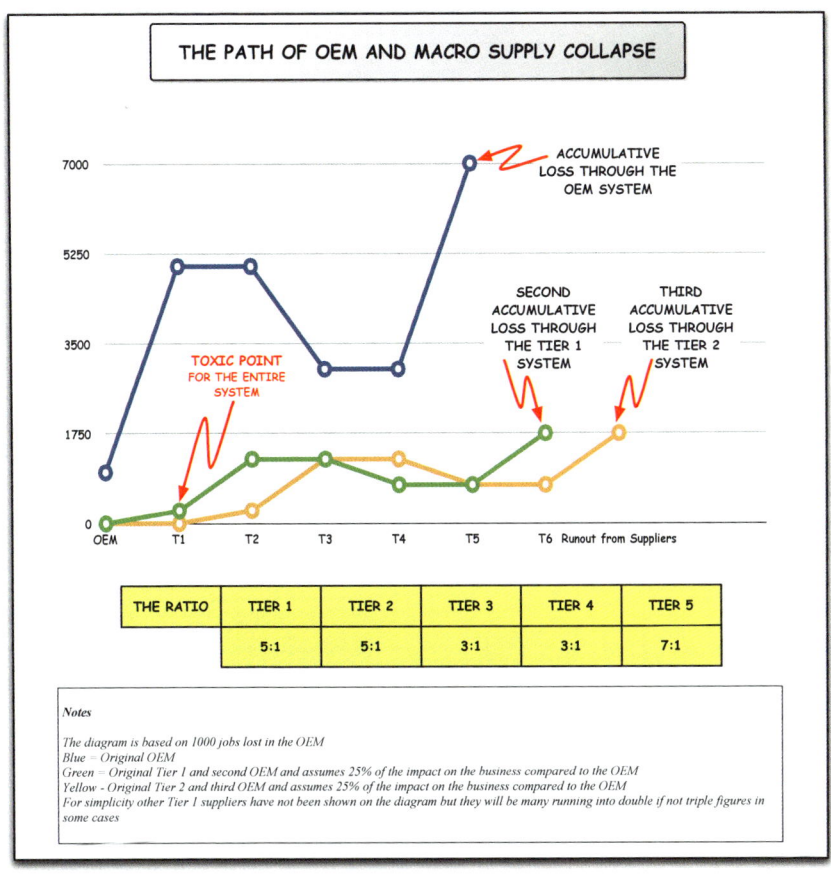

*Figure PL.4 An Example of Accumulative Job Losses In the Supply System When 1000 Jobs are Lost at an OEM*

Also consistent was the point at which the network became toxic, which is to say the point at which losses could not be stopped or reversed. The point of toxicity was not at the OEM that announced the job cuts but at the Tier 1 supplier. The Tier 1 supplier sets off a chain reaction when it sheds jobs because other suppliers start to do the same. By the time the OEM announces job cuts, the Tier 1 supplier has often already cut jobs. When the OEM announces trouble in the system, the system has, typically, already been in trouble for some time and there is nothing that can be done to stop it at that point. It seems, however, that any support provided to try to stop the job losses is usually directed at the Tier 1 and Tier 2 suppliers. This is because these are usually large employers, larger than the OEM they are supplying in some cases and they often see themselves also as an OEM. With no end customer, however, assistance to these Tier 1 and Tier 2 suppliers cannot stop the job losses. The above diagram Figure P.4, is also theoretical in that often Tier 1 suppliers are larger employers than the OEM so actually shed more jobs. The impact of this is in an order of magnitude. For example, assuming a ratio of 10:1 Tier 1 suppliers to the original OEM, the aggregate number of affected workers based on an initial OEM reduction of 1000 workers, is then in the order of 10,852,750 (i.e. approximately one order of magnitude). This does not take into account the interconnectivity of the greater (complex) system and the interdependency of the same.

The safer strategy, but riskier political expedient, is to assist the Tier 4 and Tier 5 suppliers by investing resources to keep them operational. This provides the opportunity to develop carrier technologies - technology that can be used in multiple ways across thematic networks.

The impact of the loss of one OEM again demonstrates the degree of complexity in the b-ecosystem and the challenges of managing in such an uncertain environment. Many organisations experienced down sizing during the last crisis and this leaves an organisation with a system that is significantly different to the one it had before, both internally and externally, with the difficulties of managing change compounded by the loss of knowledge that accompanies loss of jobs.

## Skills in Decision Making

Given the depth and pattern of the crisis and its legacy for business, there is a question as to where the CEOs and CFOs of the last growth period will be able to fit their skills into the growth patterns of the future. This is because the typical CEO or CFO "inherited" a successful company that was, typically, already in an upward trajectory when they took office. Their experience of growth has often been by merger and acquisition of other successful companies and competitors or by generic growth based on an existing strong customer base and line of credit (i.e. they have been sheltered by their environment, and followed safe, predictable strategies).

An additional challenge is that a company inherited during more prosperous times may have management that is not well equipped to lead the same organisation after it has experienced significant downsizing due to a crisis. A billion dollar organisation, for example, will usually advertise for a Chief Executive Officer (CEO) with experience of running a billion dollar company. During the crisis it is possible that this organisation decreased in size and is now a 500 million dollar company with a significantly changed system. There is a suggestion that many CEO's running companies after a crisis don't have experience in running a company of the size that they are left with, which means that they will make decisions on flow, structure, position and on the future, based on expectations or assumptions and an understanding of an organisation that simply isn't there anymore. While the numbers on which they base their assumptions will invariably be correct, the decisions, based on assumptions and an understanding of a different organisational structure, could be very wrong. This, in turn, contributes to greater uncertainty and could contribute to a second or third tsunami of any crisis. As a venture capitalist stated recently, running large organisations is easy; there are a lot of resources and mistakes can be hidden. Running small organisations is incredibly difficult; there aren't any resources and everybody sees and lives a mistake.

## Large Organisations Adopting the Innovative Behaviour of Small Organisations

The next generation of CFO and CEO will have to take a business that has been decimated and rebuild it, almost from scratch, as the conditions allow. This takes a different skill set to managing an already successful company. One only needs to consider the number of CEOs and CFOs of merging companies that have been ousted by their shareholders when the realization dawns that they don't have the capability to consolidate the two, or more, businesses effectively. Indeed, in postulating the uncertainty and potential risk unleashed in many "safe companies" currently, there is some concern that this is now a very different environment and those who could manage "squares" have no concept of how to successfully manage "triangles".

The next growth cycle is likely to see big business adopting the behaviour of entrepreneurs and managers of smaller businesses who grow their businesses by being intimately acquainted with how businesses start from the ground up, the flow through the business and the interrelation of their business to its b-ecosystem. The typical new profile may be more likely to be that of CEO and CFO's of larger businesses taking on the persona of a new start-up, rather than managing by the practices traditionally associated with their role in an existing large company. This is partly because new start-ups embrace practical growth dynamics and partially because of the inherent agility in a new start-up (see Figure PL.5).

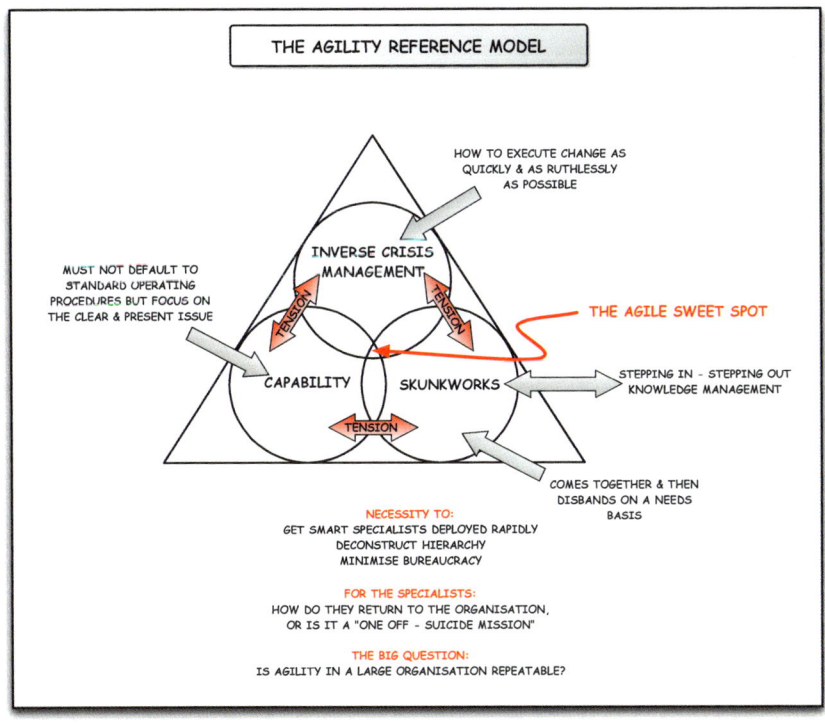

*Figure PL.5 - The Agility Reference Model*

## Agility Tactics For Crisis Management

While conventional wisdom is that in an uncertain environment there is a correlation between an organisation's size and its chances of survival, one of the paradoxes of business is that the larger the organisation the more it becomes constrained by its own size. Larger organisations, that should have more resources, also have greater bureaucracy. Layers of decision making bureaucracy tends to be risk adverse. This slows down the decision making process and, therefore, restricts agility. When times are hard, an organisation needs to be able to respond and, as such, a company in crisis needs to develop its own agility tactics.

The concept of agility will be discussed in the next series, however, effectively, if an organisation can swap one component in and out of its system to meet a customer requirement, for example if "square" can become "triangle", the system is configurable. If the system's stable configuration has the capability to reconfigure to flexibly accommodate a higher number of alternatives to meet customer requirements, so "square" can become "triangle" or "circle", the system is agile. It is important to note that an agile system requires agile capability within the organisation. At the moment, the requirements seems to be for a three-way approach where the system, the organisation and crisis management skills are effective in executing change as quickly and ruthlessly as possible. In times of crisis, however, large organisations tend to default to standard operating procedures when, actually, in times of crisis, defaulting to standard operating procedures is the last thing that they should do. The crisis management skills, therefore, are a third element requiring a recognised process. This process is the concept of skunkworks, or the ultimate creativity generator.

Typically skunkworks occur in specialist areas with a range of specialists coming together. In a large organisation the expectation is that smart specialists from within the organisation would come together; rapidly deployed to deconstruct the hierarchy of the organisation and minimise bureaucracy to respond to the issue. In effect, they would be acting like a small organisation. In a large organisation the skunkworks response raises a problem in that organisational resentment of the decisions that need to be made within a crisis can make assimilation back into their previous role impossible for the specialists deployed to the skunkworks. Furthermore, the process needs to be repeatable. An ongoing tension between the skunkworks, system capability and management needs to exist to build the knowledge and capability to continue to respond to change.

**Dip Dynamics and Change Within the Business Ecosystem**

There is an expectation that after a crisis there will be linear growth. This won't happen because the need to reacquire assets, knowledge, capital, market place and a flow of works imposes a step-by-step growth pattern on recovery. It is important to realise that once Dip Dynamics has occurred, any organisation that has gone through the Slap, Balance and Reconfiguration Zones will be fundamentally different to the organisation it was before the crisis. The system has changed. The organisation has changed. "Square" has become "triangle" and a new understanding of the system that it is left and a new management approach to this system is required (see Figure PL.6).

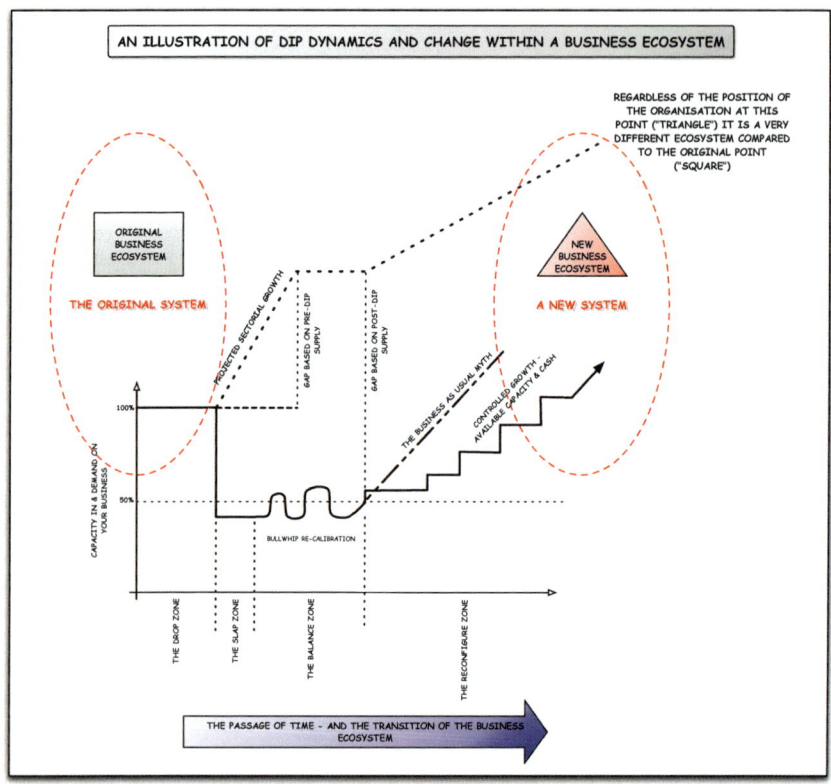

*Figure PL.6 - Dip Dynamics and the Change Within the Business Ecosystem*

No matter what the business function or the configuration of the business ecosystem, the overall emphasis is to retain customers, retain supply chain and retain competitiveness by increasing value and eliminating unnecessary waste at every opportunity and, thereby, providing tangible differentiation in aggressive markets.

"Future seeing" the market (both customer and supplier based) and designing the structure of the "new world" business is essential to success and sustainability, however, this change needs planning. Five key aspects of business leadership have been determined to be of significant importance in "future seeing" growth and resilience in business in complex adaptive systems, these are:

- Strategic supplier partnerships
- Customer relationships
- Information sharing
- Information quality
- LEAN thinking

In planning the necessary radical changes in a businesses after a crisis, it is important to consider strategically the interacting elements in the larger complex adaptive system and whether a classical, old world, operating model will apply at all.

Ideally, moving forward, there should be no single point of failure (i.e. no single partner upon whom the whole chain is reliant) and as such, the ecosystem needs to be multifaceted. This will, however, lead to increased complexity and risk, often in a time of "centralised simplification", control and risk adverse decision making.

## The Challenge of Sustainability

The crisis placed unprecedented pressures on all businesses to become leaner and smarter in the face of diminishing orders and customer bases. In many cases businesses dropped into survival mode and there was little opportunity to sustain, let alone to grow their businesses. Businesses that have been able to survive face three comparatively new yet major challenges, based on achieving mutually beneficial business and social outcomes (i.e the core principles of sustainability or triple bottom line philosophies), in addition to their ongoing operational business challenges. These three sustainability challenges are:

- Social Responsibility

- Fiscal Responsibility

- Environmental Responsibility

These principles require long-term relationships, however, long-term thinking and doing conflicts with short-term decision making and it is often the short-term view that destroys the business, slowly but certainly.

Social responsibility occurs not only within the framework of providing ethical operations, but also the seeming paradox of providing the maximum return to shareholders. Fiscal responsibilities must also focus on returning an acceptable profit and benefit to shareholders. However, to "make money you need to spend money" and currently businesses may still be facing a significant lack of supply of cash to maintain their liquidity and be facing possible extinction. Furthermore, there is the challenge of corporate responsibility within the framework of providing a sustainable environment both from a business (i.e. still remaining viable and operational) and an ecological (i.e. respecting and preserving natural resources) point of view.

These three highly constrained challenges demand new thinking in terms of business measurement and new thinking in terms of the reward structure for all the stakeholders, if there is to be any legacy to hand over in the future.

The realisation that business performance and ethics is measured from a global perspective is as alarming as it is enlightening. There is not a business in the world that is not affected by globalisation and, as such, practices in one country are easily transported into a second. The duality of ethics and business principles practiced over the last decade or so, for example by moving to low cost countries and/or reducing the duty of care to the employees in an emerging economic region, is not acceptable in the eyes of the customer and society and, as such, places huge pressures on the business to find innovative solutions to remain competitive that are both ethical and sustainable in the eyes of the market.

**Technology is Not a Differentiator**

From the early 1980's industry has seen significant and indeed unprecedented growth in technology from both a "computer generated" stance and from a process improvement stance. However, in line with the move of globalisation, the effect of the global economic crisis and indeed supplier selection and retention policies, it has become apparent, all too late for many, that technology can be bought and sold anywhere, moved and installed in comparatively short periods of time and, of itself, does not represent a significant competitive advantage or service differentiator.

Indeed investment in more (and similar) capital equipment to drive economies of scale might be the last death knell for many businesses because overheads will increase but differentiation will proportionally decrease, as companies mindlessly pursue a cost focus strategy and join the "race to the bottom" to become the lowest price provider and join the grey middle ground of product and service mediocrity that a volume and price strategy dictate. Standard information technology solutions, selected for their low perceived risk, drive organisations to design and operate the same processes and to the middle ground of mediocrity.

If we accept the premise that technology of itself does not provide significant competitive advantage, then where can an alternative and favourable advantage come from? Business processes such as LEAN systems, in appropriate environments, linked with the ability to differentiate a product or service in the market place are critical in terms of companies being able to compete and survive in globally competitive market places.

In other-words, it is not the tool but how it is used by the master craftsman that makes the difference and, as such, if a company's sustaining principle is its commitment to, and continued investment in its people (its workers, suppliers and customers), then that company must accept that it must source, install, commission and continue to maintain its human assets as it would logically do with any other capital asset within the organisation.

*The underlying core attribute of business sustainability and true differentiation remains its people.*

## The Development of Innovative People is Critical for Sustainability

When the above quote is considered within the broader aspects of sustainability it becomes apparent that the two polar views regarding training and education, where one seeks to grow and prosper within the applied environment and the other seeks to grow and prosper within the theoretical environment, are actually threatening the sustainability of both business and, indeed, the educational base that should in many respects be there to supply business with the people it needs at the level, competence and relevance that business, (i.e. the customer), needs them.

An appropriate pathway for the development of highly qualified, technically astute and managerially skilled people needs to be developed for the sustainability of business and for the sustainability of an appropriate educational framework. What is needed is a newer way of thinking where education and professional accreditation can be linked logically and where quality education can be delivered by those with meaningful industrial experience.

## Where We Are Today

Post the crisis and for those who managed to survive, the initial stop (first wave) in flow caused by Dip Dynamics is over for most businesses in most parts of the world. We have seen the rapid fall of business opportunity compared to what it was before the crisis. Moving forward, some sectors are already feeling the effect of the second tsunami and, as predicted, the availability of cash to grow business, the availability of skilled workforce to support that business and indeed the availability of sustainable customers (i.e. those with the demand and the ability to pay) are still tentative and/or non existent in some cases. This, in turn, will cause further tremors in the b-ecosystem, any one of which could erupt into another significant seismic event.

Whereas nearly every textbook would tell us that strategic partnerships and alliances should be able to overcome some of the problems described above, it becomes logical to assume that the concept of partnership needs to be redefined and the concept of nurturing the b-ecosystem taken seriously.

Furthermore, when many companies seek to outsource their products or services to offset internal risk, then the primary customer ceases to be able to satisfy their own business needs and, as such, places their own future at risk simply because their suppliers no longer have the critical mass or intense knowledge capital to deliver as they once did. This risk may factor in recent, large scale product recalls. Cost cutting exercises, such as the retrenchment of technically superior quality and operations professionals, may leave a time bomb in the business that is likely to explode just at the point of operational re-growth.

Many businesses are still operating within a false framework or belief set that suggests a growth in sales is all the business will need to get back to where it was a couple of years ago. Unfortunately, business dynamics is somewhat more complex and managing that growth and providing a measurable differentiated position places huge challenges on the business now and well into the future.

Aligning the elements of the b-ecosystem is likely to be a generational issue. The need for measurable differentiation to sustain business into the future is likely to result in perhaps the most significant supply gap of the next 20 years (i.e. the supply of appropriate and qualified natural talent). This, in turn, is likely to regress or destroy business opportunity and viability which in turn will place significant pressures on organisations, further destabilising business.

An extreme view could be that this might increase prices and thereby generate global inflation and subsequently drive a second global recession. For many, this might appear to be an alarmist thought but, then, a few years ago the first global recession was unthinkable.

## The New Beginning - Managing Business on the Edge

To have "an edge" is a term often used to describe having an advantage. In ecology, edges also refer to places where different systems meet, such as where land meets water. On the edges there is exchange and, consequently, diversity, resilience and change.

To maintain an edge - to have an advantage and to grow, an organisation must change.

The change must be a process of improvement, with unnecessary waste in the b-ecosystem constantly being reduced while value to the customer is continually being added.

To have a change process of continual improvement, an organisation must understand where the organisation is now and how its b-ecosystem works because any change will change the organisation and the b-ecosystem.

To understand where the organisation is now requires a process for gathering current knowledge about its b-ecosystem, its alignment with the other organisations in the b-ecosystem and its position in the b-ecosystem. The process needs to be iterative for constant up dating of knowledge.

The diagnostics are an iterative tool for gathering up-to-date information for knowledge about the organisation and its b-ecosystem. With up-to-date knowledge about the organisation and its b-ecosystem leaders can manage complexity to maximise competitive advantage and growth.

# References

Aggarwal, S. (1997). "Flexibility management: the ultimate strategy." *Industrial Management* 39(1): 26-31.

Bains P, Fill C and Page K (2008). *Marketing*, Oxford University Press. ISBN 978-0-19-929043-7

Ballou, R. H. (2004). *Business logistics/supply chain management* Upper Saddle River, NJ, Prentice-Hall.

Balsmeier, P. W. and W. Voisin (1996). "Supply chain management: a time-based strategy." *Industrial Management* 38(5): 24-27.

Belch G and Belch M (2007). *Advertising and Promotion, An Integrated Marketing Communications Perspective*, McGraw-Hill Irwin. ISBN-13 978-0-07-310126-2

Bell, S. (2006). *Lean enterprise systems using IT for continuous improvement*. Hoboken, New Jersey, Wiley-Interscience, A John Wiley & Sons Inc., Publication.

Blancero, D. and L. Ellram (1997). "Strategic supplier partnering: a psychological contract perspective." *International Journal of Physical Distribution & Logistics Management* 27(9/10): 616-629

Blancero & Ellram, 1997 - Blancero, D. and Ellram, L. - "Strategic supplier partnering: a psychological contract perspective". *International Journal of Physical Distribution & Logistics Management* 1997. 27 (9/10); p. 616-629

Bohme, T., Childerhouse, P., Deakins, E., Potter, A & Towill, DR (2012). Reconciling Subjectivist and Objectivist Assumptions in Management Research, *Journal of Leadership & Organizational Studies* 19:369.

Bohme, T., Childerhouse, P., Deakins, E., Potter, A & Towill, DR (2008). Why diagnosis supply chain uncertainty?, *Operations Managment,* Vol. 34 No. 3.

Boyer K and Verma R (2010). *Operations and Supply Chain Management for the 21st Century*, South-Western Cengage Learning. ISBN-13: 978 0-618-74933-1

Burgess, R. (1998). "Avoiding supply chain management failure: lessons from business process re-engineering." *International Journal of Logistics Management* 9(1): 15-23.

Buzan, T (2005). *MindMap Handbook*, Thorsons, Harper Colins. ISBN 978-0-00-720598-1

Carr, N.G (2003), IT Doesn't Matter, *Harvard Business Review, May*. <https://hbr.org/2003/05/it-doesnt-matter>

Carter C and Rogers D (2008). A Framework of Sustainable Supply Chain Management: Moving Toward New Theory, *International Journal of Physical Distribution & Logistics Management*, Emerald Group Publishing limited, Vol. 38, No 5, pp 360 - 387

Christopher, M (2009). Reducing Complexity and Improving Agility in the Supply Chain, *Supply Chain Perspectives*, 10:3. p. 29.

Claycomb, C., C. Droge, et al. (1999). "The effect of just in-time with customers on organizational design and performance." *International Journal of Logistics Management* 10(1): 37-58.

Cohen, O., Lepore, D. (1999). *The Theory of Constraints and the System of Profound Knowledge*, The North River Press MA, USA. ISBN 0-88427-163-3

Coyle J, J, Langley Jr, C. J, Gibson, B. J, Novack, R. A, Bardi, E, J. (2008). *Supply Chain Management: A Logistics Perspective*, South-Western Cengage Learning. ISBN 13: 978-0-324-22433-7

Craig C.S and Douglas S (2005). *International Marketing Research*, John Wiley & Sons Ltd. ISBN 0-470-0109509

Crane A and Matten D (2007). *Business Ethics*, Oxford University Press. ISBN 978-0-19-928499-3.

Donlon, 1996 - Donlon, J.P. - "Maximizing value in the supply chain". *Chief Executive*, 1996. 117 (October); pp. 54-63.

Donlon, J. P. (1996). "Maximizing value in the supply chain." *Chief Executive* 117(October): 54-63.

Emmelhainz, A. Margaret, et al. (1996). "So you think you want a partner?" *Marketing Management* 5(Summer): 25-41.

Evans JR and Lindsay WM (2008). *Managing for Quality and Performance Excellence*, Thompson South Western. ISBN 978-0-324-64685-6

Evans, JR & Lindsay, WM (2005). *An Introduction to Six Sigma & Process Improvement*, Cengage Learning, CT.

Fawcett S., Ellram L. and Ogden J., *Supply Chain Management*, Pearson Prentis Hall, 2007. ISBN 0-13-101504-4

Fawcett S, Ellram L and Ogden J (2007). *Supply Chain Management, From Vision to Implementation*, Pearson Prentice Hall. ISBN 0-13-101504-4

Fletcher, JD (2009). *Good Corporate Governance and Sustainability - A Loss of Containment Issues and Asset Management Challenge*, Sydney Fellows Forum, SB360, Wiggly Tin Company. ISBN 978 144 953 0006

Fletcher, JD (2009). *The Practical Art of Risk Management* - Brisbane Fellows Forum. The Wiggly Tin Company. ISBN 978 144 959 0987

Gibilisco S (2004). *Statistics Demystified*, McGrawHill. ISBN 0-07-143118-7

Gill J and Johnson P (2010). *Research Methods for Managers*, Sage. ISBN 978-1-84787-093-3

Godin, S (2005). *Purple Cow*, Penguin Books, England.

Graco Recalls 1.5 Million Strollers After Injury Reports, *Society of Manufacturing Engineers Executive Briefing*, 21 January 2010

Gray, D (2009). quoted in Hasan,H & Kazlauskas, A., "The Cynefin Framework: putting complexity into perspective", *Being Practical with Theory: A Window into Business Research*, (2014).ed. H. Hasan, University of Wollongong, Australia.

Gunther, R. (2008). "Peter Drucker-the grandfather of marketing: an interview with Dr. Philip Kotler", *Journal of the Academy of Marketing Science*, 2009. 37:17-19. <http://link.springer.com/article/10.1007/s11747-008-0105-1#>

Gunasekaran, A., C. Patel, et al. (2001). "Performance measures and metrics in a supply chain environment." *International Journal of Operations and Production Management* 21(1/2): 71-87.

Handfield, R. B. and E. L. Nichols Jr. (1999). *Introduction to supply chain management*, Upper Saddler River, New Jersey, Prentice Hall.

Hines, T. (2006). *Supply Chain Strategies - Customer Driven and Customer Focused*, Elsevier Butterworth-Heinemann. ISBN 10: 0-7506-5551-8

Jones, C. (1998). "Moving beyond ERP: making the missing link." *Logistics Focus* 6(7): 2-7.

Jutla, D., & Ma, S (1999). WebTP: A Benchmark for Web-based Order Management Systems. *Proceedings of the 32nd Hawaii International Conference on System Science.*

Kerzner, H (2006). *Project Management - A Systems Approach*, 9th ed. John Wiley & Sons, NJ. ISBN 0471741876

Lalonde, B. J. (1998). "Building a supply chain relationship", *Supply Chain Management Review* 2(2): 7-8.

Lamming, R. (1993). *Beyond partnership: strategies for innovation and lean supply*, New York, Prentice-Hall.

Leceta, J (2009). New Customer Supplier Relationships and Foundry Technology Development, *Foundry Trade Journal*, September.

Lysons K and Farrington B (2006). *Purchasing and Supply Chain Management*, Prentice Hall. ISBN-13: 978-0-273-69438-0

Magretta, J. (1998). "The power of virtual integration: an interview with Dell computers" *Harvard Business Review* 76(2): 72-84.

Mason-Jones, R. and Towill, D. R., (1997). "Information enrichment: designing the supply chain for competitive advantage." *Supply Chain Management Review* 2(4): 137-148.

Mauch, P. (2010). *Quality Management: Theory and Application*, CRC Press, ISBN 978-1-4398-1380-5

McIvor, R. (2001). "Lean supply: the design and cost reduction dimensions." *European Journal of Purchasing and Supply Chain Management* 7(4): 227-242.

Mentzer, J. T., S. Min, et al. (2000). "The nature of inter-firm partnering in supply chain management." *Journal of Retailing* 76(4): 549-68.

Monczka, R. M., K. J. Petersen, et al. (1998). "Success factors in strategic supplier alliances: the buying company perspective." *Decision Science* 29 (3): 5553-5577.

Monczka R, Handfield R, Giunipero L and Patterson J (2009). *Purchasing & Supply Chain Management*, South-Western Cengage Learning. ISBN-13: 978-0-324-38134-4

Montgomery D, Runger G (1999). *Applied Statistics and Probability for Engineers*, John Wiley & Sons Inc. ISBN 0-471-17027-5

Mullainathan, S & Shafir, E. (2013). *Scarcity Why Having Too Little Means So Much*, Allen Lane, London.

Noble, D. (1997). "Purchasing and supplier management as a future competitive edge." *Logistics Focus* 5(5): 23-27.

Novack, R. A., C. J. Langley Jr., et al. (1995). *Creating Logistics Value: Themes for the Future,* Oak Brook, IL.

Orwell, G. (1949). *Nineteen Eighty-Four*, Secker & Warburg, London.

Porters M (1998). *Competitive Strategy: Techniques for Analyzing Industries and Competitors*, The Free Press

Rix, P. (2006). *Selling managing customer relationships*, Mc Graw Hill.

Saaksjarvi, M. (1999). In Search of Business Success on the Web: The Dilemma of Defensive Functionality. *Proc. of the 32nd Hawaii International Conference on System Science.*

Sage L (2000). *Winning the Innovation Race*, John Wiley and Sons Inc.. ISBN 0-471-33346-8

Schroeder, A. and B. Hope, G (2007). I*nformation flows in a New Zealand Sheep Meat Supply Chain.* Wellington, Idea Group Inc.
Senior B and Fleming J (2006). *Organisational Change*, Prentice Hall. ISBN 978-0-27369-598-1

Sheridan, J. H. (1998). "The supply-chain paradox." *Industry Week* 247 (3): 20-9.

Srinivasan, M. M. (2004). 1*4 Principles for Building and Managing The Lean Supply Chain*, Knoxville, Thomson Business and Professional Publishing (TEXERE).

Stein, T. and J. Sweat (1998). "Killer supply chains." *Information week* 708(9): 36-46.

Stuart, F. I. (1997). "Supply-chain strategy: organizational influence through supplier alliances." *British Academy of Management* 8(3): 223-236.

Styger LEJ and Jie, F (2009). *The Principle of Dip Dynamics and Its Effect on Future Supply Chain Strategy*. The Wiggly Tin Company. ISBN 978 144 996 797 0

Styger LEJ (2009). Re-configuration of Operational Relationships Post the Current Global Economic Crisis. *Supply Chain Perspectives* 10:3.

Styger LEJ (2009). *Perspectives on Supply Post the Global Financial Crisis - Managing the Supply and Demand of Raw Talent in High Growth Sectors Post the Economic Crisis.* The Wiggly Tin Company. ISBN 978 144 996 797 0

Styger L (2009). *Perspectives on Supply Post the Global Financial Crisis*, Wiggly Tin Company. ISBN 144 996 797 3

Styger LEJ (2009). *SB360 Lee Styger Retro Papers*, The Wiggly Tin Company. ISBN 978-144-869-6727

Tan, K. C., Kannan V.R, et al. (1998). "Supply chain management: supplier performance and firm performance." *International Journal of Purchasing and Materials Management* 34(3): 2-9.

Taylor, D. H. (1999). "Supply chain improvement: the lean approach." *Logistics Focus* 7(January-February): 14-20.

The Darwin Project, (2014). The Darwin Correspondence Project< http://www.darwinproject.ac.uk/one-thing-darwin-didnt-say>, University of Cambridge.

Tompkins, J. and D. Ang (1999). "What are your greatest challenges related to supply chain performance measurement?" *IIE Solutions* 31 6: 66.

Towill, D. R. (1997). "The seamless supply chain - the predator's strategic advantage." *International Journal of Technology Management* 14: 37-55. Toyota Issues New Recall For 2.3 Million Vehicles, *Society of Manufacturing Engineers Executive Briefing*, 22 January 2010

Vokurka, R. J. and S. O Leary-Kelly (2000). "A review of empirical research on manufacturing flexibility." *Journal of Operations Management* 18(4): 16-24.

Wikipedia, *W. Edwards Deming*, http://en.wikipedia.org/wiki/W._Edwards_Deming <accessed 5 November 2014

Womack, J. and D. Jones (1996). Lean Thinking. New York, Simon and Schuster.

Yu, Z., H. Yan, et al. (2001). "Benefits of information sharing with supply chain partnerships." Industrial Management & Data Systems 101: 114-119.

## CONTACT THE AUTHOR

To find out more about COMPLEXITY, please visit the website www.leestyger.com. Here you can access more of Lee's work on how to build a successful sustainable business.

To contact the author, please email leestyger@leestyger.com

# The Edge of

# SUBVERSITY

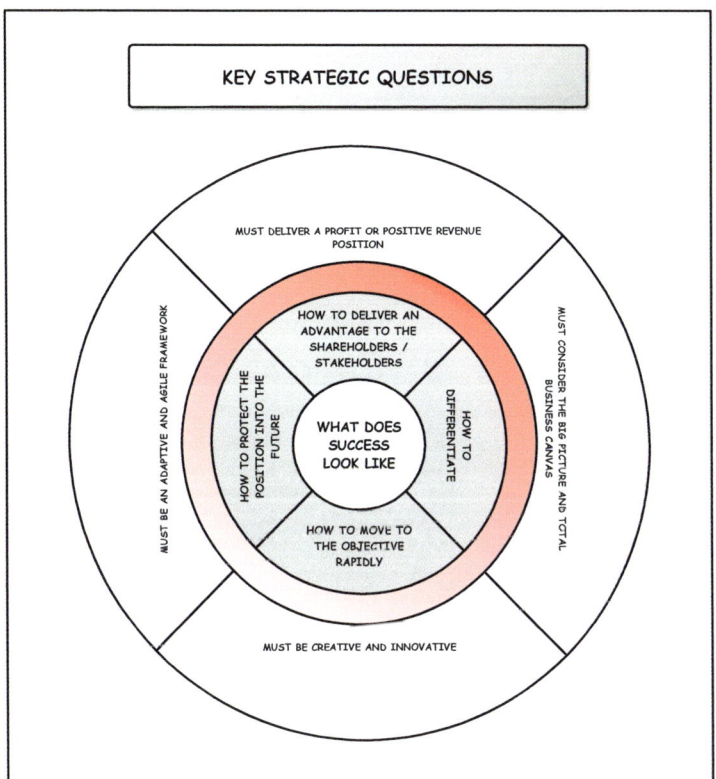

**KEY STRATEGIC QUESTIONS**

MUST DELIVER A PROFIT OR POSITIVE REVENUE POSITION

MUST BE AN ADAPTIVE AND AGILE FRAMEWORK

MUST CONSIDER THE BIG PICTURE AND TOTAL BUSINESS CANVAS

HOW TO DELIVER AN ADVANTAGE TO THE SHAREHOLDERS / STAKEHOLDERS

HOW TO PROTECT THE POSITION INTO THE FUTURE

WHAT DOES SUCCESS LOOK LIKE

HOW TO DIFFERENTIATE

HOW TO MOVE TO THE OBJECTIVE RAPIDLY

MUST BE CREATIVE AND INNOVATIVE

MANAGING BUSINESSES ON THE EDGE OF SUBVERSIVE STRATEGY

THE WORKSHOP MANUAL FOR LEADERS AND MANAGERS

# LEE E J STYGER

*Act 2 - The Next Manual in the Series*

Made in the USA
Charleston, SC
03 December 2014